MOOD FOOD

Strategies for
Contemporary Cooking and Entertaining

Hattie Ellis

HEADLINE

First published in 1998
by HEADLINE BOOK PUBLISHING

10 9 8 7 6 5 4 3 2 1

British Library Cataloguing in Publication Data
Ellis, Hattie
Mood food
1.Cookery
I.Title
641.5

ISBN 0 7472 2164 2

Typeset by
Letterpart Limited, Reigate, Surrey RH2 7BG
Printed and bound by
Butler and Tanner Ltd, Frome and London

HEADLINE BOOK PUBLISHING
A division of Hodder Headline PLC
338 Euston Road
London NW1 3BH

This book is dedicated to the testers, especially Helen and Emily; to Dad and Mum, with much love; and to Gordon, my love.

I'd like to thank my teachers at Leith's, for bringing practical knowledge to my greedy imagination; all those at *The Times* who commissioned and edited my columns, particularly Jane Owen, Tim Rice, Gill Morgan and Guy Walters; Lindsay Symons and Susan Fleming at Headline for their encouragement and skilful editing; and Eric Beaumont for his delicious illustrations.

CONTENTS

INTRODUCTION   7

WEEKDAYS

Easy-life Suppers   18

Menu: *The Dragon to Dinner*   31

Relaxed Entertaining   35

Menu: *Uninterrupted Gossip with Friends*   54

Office and Home Lunching   58

Love after Work   67

Menu: *Apparently Impetuous Seduction*   73

Health Kick   78

WEEKENDS

Saturday Night Showtime   86

CONTENTS

Menu: *Back to the Seventies Dinner*   102

Treats for Two   107

Menu: *Supper from a Corner Shop*   115

Long Sunday Lunches   120

Making a Meal out of Breakfast   134

A Revival of Afternoon Tea   141

Keeping Warm in Winter   146

Chilling Out in Summer   152

INDEX   160

INTRODUCTION

T HERE ARE TWO main aims to this book: to find ways of making truly simple, delicious food and to suit the dish to the day.

Mood, timing, guests, occasion and where you shop all play their part in what you want to eat. A relaxed supper with old friends or an impressive dinner for new ones; seduction of a new love or spoiling of Truelove; a snack snatched from a corner shop or a treat from a specialist; showtime or slob-out: they all differ as much as cheese and chips.

The book is divided into weekdays and weekends as this is a major division in how we live and, therefore, how we eat. During the week, when there is less time for cooking and shopping, easy, economical and efficient meals are the order of the day. Sometimes we are eating to exist. At the weekend, time eases and expands, giving space to enjoy cooking, eating and even shopping: perhaps you might go to a specialist shop to get some oozy cheese and a favourite wine or stray off your beaten track in the supermarket and experiment with something new.

In both the weekday and weekend sections there are menu chapters giving strategies and dishes for specific situations, be it intimidating guests, seduction, a supper made from food available in a corner shop or a long, gossipy supper with good friends.

Why Cook?

Nobody is actually obliged to cook much these days. Take-aways, deliveries, ready-meals, eating out, canteens and cheaty short-cuts can make the kitchen more a place for eating than for cooking. On one level, this feels like a liberation. On another, what an impoverishment!

Cooking is a lot about practice and experience. As you chop different kinds of tomatoes, say, from different places and in different seasons and use them in different dishes, you understand more and more through your hands, eyes, nose and mouth what makes a tomato a tomato and what it can do. However many recipe books or tv programmes there are, in the end, cooking is an endless learning process that is done empirically, by observation.

We may not have to cook these days but we can still choose to for all sorts of reasons other than obligation.

I remember once slamming out news stories on a keyboard at work and having a sudden, relieving, vision of my hands drifting through soft, white flour. Cooking after work, far from being exhausting, can be deeply relaxing. There is something in the physical absorption in cooking that is satisfying: it seems to earth some of the static of hectic, cerebral everyday living, the yakkety-yak of contemporary life. I'm not talking about three courses of fancy food, just a salad or some fish or a bit of meat and a sauce made from the pan juices, or even enjoying something good that is ready-to-eat like olives or cheese.

Some people relax and energise themselves through sport, others through gardening, but cooking is the only occupation – apart from love – that exercises all your senses. It creates a fulfilling, unselfconscious absorption in the here-and-now that you could describe as 'Zen'. And then you can eat the end product!

Many say they find cooking 'therapeutic', a concept that has become more and more ingrained in our psyche. Look after yourself, say the therapists, make sure you are mentally and physically well because the inert get crushed by the work grind and the machinations of the bottom-line merchants. Food is one way to nurture yourself, body and soul, to spend time with your lover (new or true), friends and family and to clear your space from other concerns. It is a combination of the earthy and the heavenly that is deeply nourishing.

Recipe Style

The recipes are simple. The most common laments from people who are not entirely in love with cooking is that there are 'too many ingredients' and 'it's frustrating to discover half-way through that you do not have the nth little ingredient that might make all the difference'. One of the revelations of really understanding the anatomy of a recipe is that each one has an essential core. Then there are any number of little twiddles which are not strictly necessary but there to improve the recipe by notching up the flavour bit by bit. These additions are designed by people who have a wider-than-average storecupboard at their disposal and, in the case of some restaurant recipe books, a team of *sous-chefs* and industrial equipment as well.

What I am trying to do in this book is to give the fundamentals, for the home cook, of what will work well and taste good and to keep the embellishments down to the few that make all the difference. The recipes can stand alone, as they are, when you want something truly straight-forward and tasty. It is up to you whether you want to add to or adapt them, if you like, according to your own tastes, storecupboards, experience and energy levels.

Recipes give very specific instructions, all for a purpose, yet food is also about your own likes and dislikes: an art as well as a science. Cooks vary and so do ovens. So I distributed the recipes amongst my friends and family to see how they got along with them and what variations and comments they came up with. Their comments, at the end of each recipe, are the equivalent of the scribbles that cooks often add to books at home (along with sauce splodges, in my case).

Testers

The testers were friends and family, all home cooks who enjoy food but do not have time to spend all day and night at the stove. They all had a great deal to say on what made a dish enjoyable or easy to make and how tastes and needs vary. Requests were wide: food you don't have to use your teeth for when you're feeling hungover (Petra); pasta dishes that seem luxurious and unusual, starter salads, different chicken dishes and simple puddings (Diana); food you can do most of the work for before the guests arrive (Mum); food that can be bought from M&S on the way back from work or the deli round the corner (Ed); starters that are interesting but not so complex that they require distracting, last-minute work or so big that they detract from the main course (Helen); food you can cook with a two-year-old at hand (Fresci).

Spending time with family and friends is, obviously, as much a reason for cooking as the pleasure in the food itself. Mine certainly made this book a joy to write and I'm deeply grateful for their 'feedback'.

Ingredients

Full use is made of the good ingredients now widely available but I've stayed within the parameters of the reasonably common. My own preferences and prejudices are apparent throughout the book but it seems fair to make a few of them explicit.

YUM

Booze: All bottles say 'taste me'. Everything from cider to whisky adds flavour to food. They are great storecupboard, or drinks-cupboard, ingredients. I'm particularly fond of fortified wines like sherry, Madeira and Marsala which make quick sauces and a good cook's nip.

COLOURFUL FOOD: We eat first with our eyes so contrasts and colours are really important, as are textures.

FRUIT AND VEGETABLES: I love the zoomy vitality, variety, textures and colour of good fruit and veg. A fair number of my friends are vegetarian, eat fish or enjoy meat occasionally, or consider vegetables to be at least as important as the meat or fish.

OLIVE OIL AND BUTTER: For flavour and lusciousness. Some recipes in this book do without either by using strong flavours but in others nothing else will do. Anti-fat fundamentalists forget that there is a lot of flavour in animal fats and I also tend to slosh on the olive oil. I'm not so keen on cream. A little cream can mellow and enrich a sauce but too much can make it bland.

CRISPY SKIN: Has the flavour and richness of fat and a richly savoury, caramelised surface. Carniverous cooks also know that the sweet meat near the bone makes the best pickings.

CHEESE: The best of all ready-meals. Straight-up or cooked to a melting ooze, cheese is one of the most useful, varied and easily stored ingredients.

STRONG FLAVOURS: Slow-cooked meat, chillies, onions, ginger, lemon juice and bottled sauces like soy and Worcestershire, mustards and vinegars. Marmite and ketchup. Salt and vinegar crisps.

YUK

FACTORY-FARMED MEAT: Mass-produced chicken has a strange taste and pappy texture compared to a proper free-range bird. These recipes use joints rather than pieces as they are easier to find free-range or, more economically, you can buy a whole bird and joint it yourself or get a butcher to do it for you. Mass-produced pork can be very dry and taste odd. Fattier cuts like pork belly are the best bet if buying ordinary pork, cooked until the fat is nicely gelatinous. (Good free-range pork is, of course, delicious and much under-rated. Suckling pig is outrageously good.)

OILY FISH: I know I should like this for health reasons but, to me, some of them can be iffy, not to say whiffy. I have enjoyed very fresh mackerel but it goes downhill rapidly and rancidly. Sometimes I like herrings and sometimes not. Sardines? Phooey. Tuna, fresh and canned, is my favourite oily fish and I adore other kinds of fish and all shellfish.

FILO PASTRY AND FRISÉE LETTUCE: Impossible to eat.

INSIPID TOMATOES AND OUT-OF-SEASON FRUIT: There's nothing more disappointing than biting into something that is a ghost of its true self. This includes quite a lot of tropical fruit which is often not sold at its best. Mangoes and lychees are the best bet.

Equipment, Briefly

You won't need special equipment for most of these recipes and, in nearly all cases, you won't have to weigh ingredients.

Cooking equipment is a very big subject but here are just a few tips on the basics. Heavy pans conduct heat well and stop food burning. Watch out for cheap imitations that have a heavy base and very thin sides. I'm a big fan of Woll frying pans which are deep enough for plenty of sauce and thick enough that you need minimal oil for frying. For weekday convenience, a medium-large pan with a steamer allows you to cook potatoes or pasta below and steam vegetables on top.

A big, heavy knife (I use a lovely solid Sabatier), kept sharp, makes short work out of chopping and you can use the blade to transport food to the pan. A robust metal colander with a steady base makes life easier. A potato masher can mush up other vegetables if you do not have a food processor.

I use my oven a lot, particularly when cooking for four or more, because you can put the food in an ovenproof dish and let it cook while you get on with something else. A set of shallow, ovenproof dishes gives you a range of sizes that you know will feed roughly two, four, six or eight.

Seasoning

Unconsidered seasoning is the most common flaw in cooking (I hate to state the obvious, but another one is not reading the recipe through, properly, before you start). Always use your own judgement alongside the instructions as ingredients vary greatly: cheeses and bacons have differing saltiness; one chilli can blow your socks off and make your nose run while another gives just a mild buzz. Be cautious initially, taste as you go and then adjust, after tasting again, at the end. A squeeze of lemon or, with tomato dishes, a tiny pinch of sugar or drop of honey at the end of cooking can often lift a dish if your ingredients turn out to be disappointing. A few shakes of a sauce like soy or even Worcestershire, and chopped fresh herbs work in the same way. But good old salt and pepper can also do a great deal. I use sea salt which has a nice flavour and crunch. I have not listed salt and pepper in the ingredients for each recipe, assuming you have them to hand, but you will need one or both in most savoury recipes.

Numbers

The recipes feed numbers varying from one or two to six. It is often more fun to cook for two or three (more chance to talk and less washing up) and people are always looking for something to vary their weekday standbys. The dinners are for six as this is the maximum number I personally find enjoyable to cook for. Any more and you start to get into catering.

Measurements

Measurements throughout are for rounded, not level, tablespoons and teaspoons.

I have mostly used metric measurements, although I've occasionally put in the measurement of milk in terms of pints so you can judge the quantity from a pint carton. The following table is an approximated conversion of metric to imperial measurements.

WEIGHT

Metric	Imperial	Metric	Imperial
20g	¾ oz	285g	10 oz
30g	1 oz	300g	just under 11 oz
40g	1½ oz	340g	12 oz or ¾ lb
75g	2½ oz	370g	13 oz
80g	3 oz	400g	14 oz
100g	4 oz or ¼ lb	425g	15 oz
140g	5 oz	450g	1 lb
170g	6 oz	500g	1 lb 2 oz
200g	7 oz	600g	1 lb 6 oz
225g	8 oz or ½ lb	900g	2 lb
250g	9 oz	1kg	2 lb 4 oz

VOLUME

Metric	Imperial	Metric	Imperial
5ml	1 teaspoon	200ml	7 fl oz
15ml	1 tablespoon	250ml	9 fl oz
20ml	just under 1 fl oz	500ml	18 fl oz
50ml	2 fl oz	1 litre	1¾ pints
100ml	4 fl oz		

AMERICAN MEASUREMENTS
(approximate)

1 litre : 5 cups	225ml : 1 cup	
580ml/1 pint : 2½ cups	150ml/¼ pint : ½ cup + 2 tablespoons	
300ml/½ pint : 1¼ cups	100ml : ½ cup	

flour	: 1 cup	: 140g
white sugar	: 1 cup	: 225g
butter	: 1 cup	: 225g
uncooked rice	: 1 cup	: 200g
fresh breadcrumbs	: 1 cup	: 50g

WEEKDAYS

Easy-life supper

EASY-LIFE SUPPERS

W<small>HAT'S FOR SUPPER?</small> The question asked day after day, after school, after work, rushing in before going out, hungry after coming in. Supper is the bedrock of cooking, thrown together from basic, economical ingredients bought in a weekly shop.

All of these recipes have as few ingredients as possible and the minimum number of pots to wash. For one or two, cooking in a pan is quick and easy. For four, it is often easier to put the food in the oven and let it cook while you get on with something else.

The time to start thinking about supper is often shortly before you want to eat it. Eggs make good last-minute meals like cheese or herb omelettes or *pipérade*, made by scrambling eggs with some sliced peppers that have been softened in olive oil, tomatoes and basil.

Some tinned foods are useful – beans such as flageolet beans and chickpeas that can be thrown together with tomatoes, onions, garlic and a few herbs. Some put a splash of red wine in baked beans; I believe in lots of butter and a grind of black pepper. Little cubes of cheese are good melted in hot soup.

For a different kind of starch, sweet potatoes bake in 45 minutes and are particularly tasty and healthy. Look for the ones with orange rather than white flesh (scrape away a bit of the skin in the shop to make sure). Quick-cook pasta is thin and disappointing. Dried pasta is often nicer than fresh. Pasta sauces made of tomatoes can be improved by adding a little grated orange rind or an anchovy or two, which melt into the sauce giving it a savoury note. Buy bottled anchovies, not tinned, as they are more convenient to keep in the fridge. Saffron adds fragrance and sunshine to all tomato dishes.

For a foolproof formula to cook rice, see page 45 in the Relaxed

Entertaining chapter. Bread is the fastest starch of all and a thick slice can scoop up sauce and add bulk to the meal. Most bread is made from over-treated flour and risen too quickly. Slow-risen breads, often called 'traditional' on the packet, and proper wholemeal breads fill you up and need not be heavy. They have more of a satisfying chew and flavour to them.

Spinach (the whole leaf kind, not the chopped), peas and broad beans are my preferred frozen vegetables. There are many reasons why you might want to buy organic vegetables, and organic potatoes, certainly, taste noticeably better than ordinary ones.

If you want a sweet end, fruit, yoghurt and chocolate are easy to grab. Good chocolate, with 70 per cent cocoa solids, is worth the price and, strange to say, its strength of flavour makes you want to nibble rather than guzzle. If you want more of a food hug, Dr Food Love prescribes fudge, baked apples stuffed with mincemeat and marzipan, ice-cream or the banana recipe on page 30.

One of the more unusual storecupboard stand-bys from my local Waitrose is *stinco di prosciutto*, a ham shank which can be stored in the cupboard and boils-in-the-bag in 15 minutes to give you meat that falls off the bone. I first came across it in Vivian's, an excellent and idiosyncratic deli in Richmond (tel: 0181 940 3600), which has a whole section devoted to storecupboard items that make a decent supper in a rush. Vivian has tasted his way through many, many packets and tins to find the best.

My feeling about ready-meals is that they are expensive and never as good as home-cooked food, apart from the curries which can be pretty good. Otherwise, the seasoning is usually iffy, the textures suffer and they are often laced with a large amount of salt and fat to make them palatable. Are they really worth the loss of taste, freshness and money? The main pleasure is that of revelling in super-slobbery rather than the taste of the food itself. So yes, once in a while, accompanied by bought garlic bread, a bottle of wine and some deep sofa-burrowing in front of the tv followed by long phone calls to your best friends. But as a daily diet, not for me.

I make no apology for the simplicity of the dishes in this chapter. Supper is not about being challenged. Here's to baked potatoes, fish fingers, sausages, tuna melts and baked beans. Familiarity, in food, breeds comfort not contempt.

Pasta with Roasted Aubergine, Tomato and Red Onion Sauce

This was designed as a 'soap-opera supper' so the pasta cooks in the first half of *Coronation Street* and is thrown together with the sauce in the commercial break to be eaten in front of the tv during the second half.

For tv dinners that are eaten on your lap rather than a table, try to find food that can be served in a bowl and eaten with just a fork or in your hands. Nothing too sloppy that can spill and nothing that requires looking down or cutting while your eyes want to be glued to the box.

Serves two

large aubergine :	approx. 350-400g
olive oil :	3-4 tablespoons
tomatoes :	4
red onion :	1
dried pasta :	160g
balsamic vinegar :	1-2 teaspoons to taste

1   About 40 minutes before you want to eat, preheat the oven to 190°C fan oven/200°C or 400°F electric oven/Gas 6. Cover a baking tray with foil.
2   Cut the aubergine into 1cm cubes. Put at one end of the lined baking tray and toss in 2-3 tablespoons olive oil. Spread them out in a single layer.
3   Cut the tomatoes into quarters. Peel and slice the red onion. Put the

tomatoes and onion at the other end of the baking tray to the aubergines. Slosh some more olive oil over the tomatoes and onions. Season all the vegetables with salt and plenty of black pepper. Put in the oven for 30 minutes. Put a large pan of salted water on to boil.

4   Following the general rule for pasta, use shapes for this chunky sauce (strands are better suited to thin sauces). Put the pasta in the pan and cook according to packet instructions or until al dente (usually 8-10 minutes).

5   Briefly drain the pasta and put in two large bowls or plates. Mix the roasted vegetables together with the balsamic vinegar. Put on top of the pasta and serve.

COMMENTS

Fresci: An easy, warming, rustic pasta dish.

Johnny and Marina: Cooked it for five as a supper dish, using 2 large aubergines, 12 tomatoes and 3 onions and added a red pepper. Used wholewheat penne. Put the pasta in an enormous bowl in the middle of the table for people to help themselves. A great success.

Emma: Delicious and easy. Even ultra-carnivorous husband liked it (with sausages on the side). Also good with fish.

Ever-ready Carbonara

An ultra-quick version of spaghetti carbonara using fridge stand-bys like Parma ham and Parmesan. *Crème fraîche* keeps longer in the fridge than ordinary cream.

Serves any number but best done for one to three

dried spaghetti/tagliatelle : 80-100g per person
spring onions : 1 per person
Parma ham : 2 slices/30g per person
Parmesan : 1-2 tablespoons grated
per person
eggs : 1 per person
crème fraîche/Greek yoghurt : 1 tablespoon per person

1   Put a pan of water on to boil. Measure out the pasta (about a 1p coin's diameter of tagliatelle or spaghetti per person) and cook according to packet instructions or until al dente (usually 8-10 minutes).

2   Meanwhile, finely slice the white and green of the spring onion and cut the Parma ham into strips. Grate the Parmesan.

3   When the pasta is cooked, drain briefly and put back in the pan. Crack 1 or more eggs into the pasta and add the rest of the ingredients. Mix into the pasta. The residual heat of the pasta may cook the eggs enough but, if not, turn the heat on to low and stir for 30 seconds – 1 minute, or more, until the egg is cooked. Season with plenty of freshly ground black pepper.

4   Serve immediately on its own or with a green salad.

COMMENTS

Patti: Good, quick and different. I find raw spring onions
a bit too assertive but you could stir-fry them very quickly to
soften their taste.
Katherine: Ate this after a drinks party and used lardons instead
of Parma ham. Good with a green salad.

Cod with Leek and Cider Sauce

Cod would be my top choice for this recipe but you can substitute it with any white fish fillet such as haddock, hoki, coley or whatever else is cheapest and freshest on the day.

Fresh fish has the best texture but, if you want to eat fish a few days after your weekly shop, frozen fish is convenient (and supermarket fish counters often sell defrosted fish in any case). You can defrost frozen fish in a microwave or on a plate in the fridge during the day.

Serves two

leek : 1 medium
butter : large knob
skinned white fish fillet : 400g
cider : 150ml

1 Slice the leek thinly. Melt the butter in a pan over a low heat. Turn up the heat and add the leeks. Stir-fry for a minute then push to the side of the pan.

2 Add the fish to the pan and fry over a high heat for 2 minutes on each side. You may need to stir the leeks to ensure they do not burn.

3 Add the cider and let it bubble away for 2 minutes until the sauce has reduced and the cod is cooked all the way through. If it needs more time and the sauce is getting too thick, add a little water or more cider.

4 Serve with potatoes or pasta and one other vegetable.

COMMENTS

Emily: Mustard seeds would be good in the sauce.
Susan: Used skinned chicken breast instead of fish and cooked it

for longer. Loved the leek and cider combination.
Marinate the chicken in the cider first.

Patti: Gorgeous. Almost like a meat sauce in its strength.
Worked well for two but not when doubled for four as you can't
get enough heat in the pan to reduce the sauce properly.
Good with a bit of cream.

Helen: Quick and very tasty. I often find fishy things get
a bit dry but this was melt-in-the-mouth.

Frog-and-Toad-in-the-Hole

A variation on the traditional toad-in-the-hole using courgettes as 'frogs'
alongside the sausage 'toads'. This dish allows you (and any children) to
play a bit, arranging the vegetables and sausages in the batter or throwing
them in willy-nilly.

Serves four

plain flour	100g
eggs	2
milk	150ml
water	150ml
pork sausages	8
cherry tomatoes	12
courgette	1 medium
vegetable or olive oil	1 tablespoon

1   Preheat the oven to 200°C fan oven/220°C or 425°F electric oven/Gas 7.
Put the flour, eggs, milk, water and some salt and pepper in a food
processor bowl and whizz to get a smooth batter.

If doing this by hand, put the flour in a bowl with some salt and pepper, crack the eggs into the middle of the flour and gradually draw the flour into the eggs using a whisk or wooden spoon whilst adding the milk and water a bit at a time until you have a smooth batter.

2   If you want the sausages to be browned all over, fry one side over a high heat until brown. Cut the cherry tomatoes in half. Cut the courgette into 1cm thick slices.

3   Put the oil in an ovenproof dish or roasting tin and heat it in the oven for a couple of minutes. Pour the batter into the tin and arrange the sausages, tomatoes and courgette slices in the batter, being as artistic, ordered or random as you wish.

4   Put in the oven for 40 minutes, until the sausages are browned and parts of the batter crisp and brown.

5   Serve with green vegetables or a salad.

COMMENTS

Fresci: Infinitely more impressive to look at than your average toad. Good fun and easy to make, even with a wicked two-year-old boy to 'help' (he kept trying to put the egg shells in as well as the tomatoes).

Katherine: The tomatoes are a good addition. Browned the sausages on one side first. It's okay to serve it without any other vegetables, on its own.

Sausages with Grainy Mustard Mash and Roasted Parsnips

There are two tricks in this recipe. Firstly, it is easier and less wasteful to peel potatoes after they have been cooked, than before. Secondly, it is far easier to cook lots of sausages in the oven than to stand over them spluttering in a pan.

This dish goes very well with red cabbage. As a sweeter alternative to vinegar and sugar, I like to cook a sliced, medium cabbage (about 1kg) with 400ml cider or apple juice and 4 tablespoons redcurrant jelly.

Serves four

pork sausages	:	12
parsnips	:	3 medium/about 400g
olive oil	:	1 tablespoon
potatoes	:	2-3 large/700g
butter	:	50g
grainy mustard	:	2 tablespoons
milk	:	150ml

1   Preheat the oven to 190°C fan oven/200°C or 400°F electric oven/Gas 6. Put the sausages on a baking tray and put in the oven for 30-40 minutes, until browned.

2   Meanwhile, peel the parsnips and cut into finger-sized pieces. Put in an ovenproof dish or baking tray and toss in the olive oil, with some salt and pepper. Put in the oven with the sausages for 30 minutes or until brown on the outside and cooked right through.

3   Wash but don't peel the potatoes, cut into chunks, put in a pan of salted water and bring to the boil. Simmer until tender, about 15-20

minutes. Drain and leave for a couple of minutes until cool enough to handle. The peel comes away easily.

4   Put the drained potatoes in a food processor bowl with the butter, grainy
mustard, milk and a large pinch of salt. Process to a mash, or use a potato masher.

5   Serve the sausages with the potatoes, parsnips and a green vegetable or red
cabbage.

COMMENTS

Susan: Used venison sausages to add a touch of exoticism.
Sarah: Mixed sliced leeks into the mash, which was good.

Lamb Chops in a Spicy Redcurrant Gravy

The nicest bits of chops are the little bits of meat you have to gnaw off
the bone.

Serves two

olive oil :	½ tablespoon
lamb chops :	2 or 3 each
water :	2 small wine glasses/200ml
redcurrant jelly :	1½ tablespoons
Worcestershire sauce :	couple of shakes

1   Heat the oil in a frying pan over a high heat. Season the chops on one
side with salt and pepper and put them, seasoned-side down, in the pan.
Cook for 3 minutes, or until well browned. Do not worry if it seems to
be getting very brown: browning meat properly gives it lots of flavour.

2   Season the other side and turn over. Cook for another 2-3 minutes, until

brown. Balance the chops, fat-side-down, at the edge of the pan to brown the fat on the bone.

3 Lay the chops flat and add the water (it will bubble up furiously) and the redcurrant jelly to the pan. Let it bubble away for 3-5 minutes, stirring to melt the jelly.

4 Cut into a chop to check it is as you like it and cook for longer if necessary, adding a little more water if the sauce becomes too reduced and looks like burning. It should reduce enough to become slightly syrupy. Add the Worcestershire sauce, to taste. Put the chops on serving plates and pour over the gravy.

5 Serve the lamb with something like mashed potatoes and peas or steamed greens to mop up the glossy gravy.

COMMENTS

Isa and Mark: Delicious. If serving at a dinner party it could be smartened up with fresh redcurrants or herbs.

Herby Potato and Tomato Gratin

Goes well with cold meat, or you could put some cheese in the middle to make a complete vegetarian dish. A tablespoon of capers is a nice addition, if you have them.

Serves five to six as a side dish, four for a main dish

cooked potatoes : 8 medium
parsley : 2-3 tablespoons chopped
garlic : 2 cloves
tapenade/black olives : ½ tablespoon/8

lemon : ½
tomatoes : 6
olive oil : 3 tablespoons
cheddar cheese or
mozzarella (optional) : 100g
capers (optional) : 1 tablespoon

1   Preheat the oven to 190°C fan oven/200°C or 400°F electric oven/Gas 6. Cut the cooked potatoes (you can use leftover roast or boiled potatoes) into 1cm slices. Finely chop a large bunch of parsley to get about 2-3 tablespoons of chopped leaves. Crush the garlic. Cut the black olives into small pieces. Grate the rind off the half lemon. Mix the parsley, garlic, olives and lemon rind together. Slice the tomatoes.

2   Pour a tablespoon of the olive oil over the bottom of a shallow ovenproof dish. Layer up: half the potatoes; a seasoning of salt and pepper; the parsley/garlic/olive/lemon mixture; the sliced tomatoes; cheese and capers (if using them). Top with the rest of the potatoes, being tidy or messy according to occasion, mood or temperament.

3   Season with more salt and pepper and trickle over the remaining tablespoons of olive oil. Put in the oven for 30 minutes until the top is browned.

4   Serve the potato and tomato gratin warm or hot.

COMMENTS

Aidan and Jenny: This dish has become a favourite of ours. Very easy to prepare, unusual and tasty. The potatoes really soak up the flavours and the olives, garlic and lemon complement each other. We use allotment potatoes with their skins and serve it with a green salad as a main dish. Aidan recommends hot horseradish mustard as well.

OJ Bananas

Bananas are nature's convenience food, in funky packaging that puts manufacturers to shame. You can have them around the house ready for on-the-hoof breakfasts, snacks and impromptu puddings like this. Orange juice seems to bring out the flavour of bananas.

Serves any number

bananas : 1 per person
raisins : 1 tablespoon per person
orange juice : 1 tablespoon per person
(an average orange produces
4 tablespoons juice)
rum/Cointreau (optional) : ½ tablespoon per person

1 Preheat the oven to 190°C fan oven/200°C or 400°F electric oven/Gas 6.
2 Peel the bananas. Put each banana in the centre of a piece of foil large enough to wrap generously around it. Scatter a tablespoon of raisins over each one. Gather up the foil and pour orange juice into each parcel and, if you like, the rum or Cointreau as well.
3 Seal the parcels completely. Put the bananas on a baking tray (just in case any juice spills out) and put in the oven for 15 minutes.
4 These keep warm in their sealed packets while you eat the main course.

COMMENTS

Isa and Mark: Used Cointreau and raisins. Delicious. Could easily be used as a recipe for children with just orange juice.

careful - the plates are cold.

MENU:

The Dragon to Dinner

MULLED LAMB
LUXURIOUS FRUIT TART

Serves the dragon and five humans

Your intimidating mother-in-law (or mother) is coming to dinner mid-week to cast her beady eye on your cooking and household mismanagement.

Do not be a hostage to fortune: cook the food the night before. You'll have to stay in anyway, to clean the house and do those panicky extras, like putting out new J-cloths.

Choose a dish which is classy but not extravagant so she cannot sniff disapprovingly at your profligacy. A two-course meal is quite long enough.

Invite other people. There is safety in numbers and, you never know, it may just be your in-law relationship that creates the tension. She may be utterly charming to strangers.

Before dinner, dose her with just the right amount of her favourite tipple to make her mellow but not belligerent or maudlin.

Follow the stew with an expensive and smart fruit tart which you have ordered your partner to get: nobody should be allowed to shirk total responsibility for their parents.

Mulled Lamb

Spiced scents warm the air as the meat in this lip-smacking stew cooks to tenderness. This dish is also very good on cold days or as a dish you can leave in the oven so it is ready when you come home hungry after a walk or drink at the pub.

Serves six

onions : 2
olive oil : 1 tablespoon
plain flour : 2 tablespoons
dried apricots : 20/125g
red wine : 2 small wine glasses/200ml
water : 300ml
orange : 1
cloves : 4
cinnamon sticks : 2
lamb shoulder chops : about 1.4kg

1　Preheat the oven to 170°C fan oven/180°C or 350°F electric oven/Gas 4. Slice the onions and soften for 5 minutes in the oil in a large casserole dish. Meanwhile, cut the shoulder chops into chunks, removing the bone.

2 Stir the flour into the onions for a minute then turn the heat off and add the apricots, wine and water.

3 Cut the orange in half and stick the cloves into the peel of both halves. Add them to the pot with the cinnamon sticks. Add the lamb. Season with salt and pepper.

4 Cook for 2½-3 hours or until the meat is meltingly soft, making a deliciously rich sauce.

5 If making this the night before, let it cool and then put in the fridge. The fat rises to the top in the fridge and you *can* take all or some of it off, but I would leave it all in. Remove any cloves or cinnamon stick you can spot. Reheat the next evening in the oven or on the hob.

6 That evening, do a final panic check of decency of house and self and check that Truelove has bought tart. Put it on a nice plate. Make some mashed potato or throw some potatoes in the oven to bake. You can rub the surface with a little olive oil to make them glossy.

7 Settle the dragon down with some salted cashews and a big gin. At this stage, if you start to crack, you can disappear into the kitchen and pretend to be busy.

8 Sit the dragon next to the most charming guest and her beloved offspring. Place yourself down at the other end of the table on the pretext of being near the kitchen. Serve the stew with the potato and some baby spinach leaves or steamed Savoy cabbage to mop up the juices. Be careful not to give the dragon any stray cloves or cinnamon stick.

9 Get Truelove to serve tart. Congratulate yourself on being a dutiful home-maker.

COMMENTS

Susan: Good with baked potatoes.
Frances: Added 2 cloves of garlic which added a nice extra flavour.
I like the ease of preparation of the dish (no browning of the

meat required) and the lack of attention it needed whilst
in the oven. Very tender lamb.
Johnny: Ate it with mashed swede.
Nicky: I like this because, brought up on traditional English cooking,
the combination of fruit and meat seems rather sinfully exotic.

RELAXED ENTERTAINING

BEAUMONT

O NCE UPON A TIME meals arrived as regularly as a clock's hands
to the appointed hour. Nowadays, weekday suppers do not run like
clockwork. The guests? Some early, most late by varying degrees. The
number of guests? Fluctuating up to the moment you put the food on the
table. The cook? Late home from work and then distracted by a long but
unavoidable phone call.

Don't give up on weekday entertaining: it seems a shame to let the day
rule the night. Just adapt your approach to suit the circumstances. The
following strategies enable you to spend time with the guests rather than
be stranded in the kitchen feeling like a dirty dish-cloth and wishing they
would all go home.

First of all, do not set yourself up by aiming to do more than is possible and enjoyable. Now that good ingredients are widely available, you
can buy some of the food all ready to eat. Convenience does not have to
be a cheat if you shop intelligently. Look at cheese, the ultimate ready-
meal. The cow, the cheese-maker and the shop-owner have done all the

work for you. Concentrate your cooking effort on the main course and serve ready or almost-ready foods for the other courses. Ice-cream, cured meats, dips, breads and biscuits just need shopping and packet-opening skills. On a weekday it is more important to give people good, simple food quickly than elaborate creations slowly. The recipes in this chapter make use of widely available foods that need little or no preparation and most of the ingredients can be bought at a weekly shop and kept in the fridge until you want to use them.

If you are going to cheat completely, do it with style. I once arrived for a weekday dinner at the same time as the host leapt out of a taxi, in a tutu of M&S bags. We chatted and had a first drink as he snipped and shoved and seasoned. When all was done, in under 5 minutes, his wife came gliding down the stairs with freshly washed hair. The meal worked because it started with generous platefuls of smoked salmon (which just goes to show that you can hug corners in flash cars).

A good mid-week tactic is to take the first course off the table and serve it with drinks, so nobody has to wait hungrily for late-comers and the whole meal does not drag on for hours.

For the main course and the pudding, put the food out on serving plates for people to help themselves. Not only does this save the cook some palaver, it also means guests can eat as much or as little as they want. Appetites are much harder to gauge on weekdays than the weekend. How can you know who has had a heavy work lunch, who is dieting or who ate a stop-gap cheese sandwich after work?

The trickiest part of mid-week entertaining is when you are longing to get to bed and your guests are settling in with the whisky bottle. Yawning does not always work, especially if they are, as you hope they are, having a good time. It helps if you start the whole meal as early as you can, asking people to come early, straight from work, around 7.30pm or even 7pm rather than after 8. People tend to want to leave earlier too and, if not, it seems less churlish to do a friendly chuck-out, apologising with a big sleepy smile any time after 11.30pm. Starting the washing up scatters people like a bad smell. Moving the conversation towards the mundanities of what everyone is up to the next day is a good trick. More blatantly, ask everyone what time they get up. If you are entertaining as a couple, one partner going off to bed is verging on the rude but a definite prompt. My parents have a story about a woman who would get up and physically move on the hands of the clock when it was time for her guests to go.

In the end, any of these tactics (apart from the clock) are okay because mid-week entertaining has to be informal to be worthwhile. The whole mood is about being with people and having enough to drink and eat rather than showing off, elaborate social engineering, etiquette minuets and spending hours at the stove and table. It is soul music not grand opera.

Food with the First Drink

Anyone reeling from a busy day urgently needs food, drink and a chair, now. Give your friends something to eat with the first drink. A bowl of peanuts or crisps is not ideal: I always eat too many, on automatic, and then suddenly feel sick. Serve something more appealing, and include some fresh food, to blunt the edge of hunger.

Here are some ready and almost-ready prepared foods that should do the trick.

NACHO CHIPS and READY-PREPARED VEGETABLES with bought DIPS or GUACAMOLE. To make an almost-instant DIP, mix soured cream with an equal amount of mayonnaise and add a crushed ½ clove of garlic or some Worcestershire sauce and a good squeeze of lemon.

CURED MEATS like *chorizo* sausage, *bresaola* (Italian cured beef) and Parma ham on slices of plain or olive-oil drizzled CIABATTA and a bowl of RADISHES.

BREAD STICKS (I like the ones with sesame seeds) and CHEESE STRAWS and a bowl of CHERRY TOMATOES and MOZZARELLA balls or chunks mixed with torn-up BASIL leaves. Never keep tomatoes in the fridge: it chills down their flavour.

Two different kinds of OLIVES and fingers of PITTA BREAD to dip into one or more of the following: TARAMASALATA, HOUMOUS, TZATZIKI and AUBERGINE PURÉE.

Warmed ONION BHAJIAS, either cocktail-sized or larger ones cut into quarters, to be dipped, if you like, in YOGHURT. Bhajias are generally of a better quality than samosas.

Nutty, filling OATCAKES or squares of TOAST spread with CREAM CHEESE or a SOFT or SEMI-SOFT CHEESE that is easy to spread, like Taleggio.

Halved CHERRY TOMATOES or cold NEW POTATOES with a dab of PESTO or, to smarten up the new potatoes, soured cream or mayonnaise and FISH ROE.

Chunks of SMOKED TROUT on slices of *baguette* spread with a dollop of mayonnaise and a dab of HORSERADISH SAUCE.

To make BRUSCHETTA: put thick slices of bread into the preheated oven at 190°C fan oven/200°C or 400°F electric oven/Gas 6 until crisp. Rub with a cut clove of garlic, if you like, and drizzle with olive oil. Top with ingredients like chopped hard-boiled egg, mayonnaise and dill; toasted pine kernels and cottage cheese spiked with a little horseradish sauce; mozzarella melted over capers or a simple spreading of tapenade decorated with fresh green herbs such as chervil or basil.

Use the Spanish method of rubbing a cut TOMATO and clove of garlic over toasted bread then drizzle with olive oil and add simple toppings like CHEESE or CURED HAM.

SMOKED FISH PÂTÉ (see below) made quickly the night before or that evening, spread on crackers.

Smoked Fish Pâté

Smoked trout is particularly good in this simple dish. Make it by hand or in a food processor, as you like.

Serves six as a starter

smoked trout or mackerel : **150g**
spring onions : **2-3 to taste**
cream cheese : **300g**
lemon : **good squeeze or two**

1 Mash up the trout or mackerel, picking out any bones. Slice the spring onions.
2 Mix the onions and cream cheese with the fish. Season with lemon juice and black pepper, to taste.
3 Serve on oatcakes, crackers or toast.

COMMENTS

Petra and Paddy: The general consensus was feverish.
Cousin Alex said incredulously, 'This is better than my Mum's';
others commented, 'Incredibly good and unusually light'.
Used smoked mackerel. We started picking out the bones but
didn't get very far as we quickly hit upon the notion of smashing
them into tiny pieces, thus neutralising their choking capacity,
in the food processor. We put the rest of the ingredients
in there too. Why not?

Feta and Mint Salad

When in a dashing hurry, use ingredients that are easy to cut or can be crumbled or torn in your hands, like feta and mint. This starter can be made before the guests arrive. Use bagged ready-prepared mixed salad leaves to make it ultra-quick. A nice addition is some roughly chopped coriander to get the refreshing Vietnamese combination of coriander and mint.

Serves six to eight as a large starter, four for a lunch dish

mint :	large handful
prepared mixed salad leaves :	400g
feta cheese :	400g
lemon :	½
olive oil :	3 tablespoons

1 Roughly chop the mint leaves. Mix with the salad leaves, in a serving bowl.
2 Crumble the feta roughly in your hands to make rough 1cm cubes. Scatter over the salad.
3 Just before serving, dress with the lemon juice and olive oil and some black pepper.

COMMENTS

Petra and Paddy: Used Sainsbury's herb salad, rocket, mint and coriander. Delicious. The mint made all the difference. Our resident foodie, Nick, said that he was deeply moved by the fact that such an incredibly simple mix of ingredients could deliver such fabulous flavours. The sublimely uncomplicated salad dressing led him to express himself in cliché: 'Less is more.'

Frances: One of the guests suggested adding black olives.
I felt there were enough flavours already. A substantial starter that
would make a good light lunch dish with some crusty bread.

Chicken or Fish with Baked New Potatoes

For an ultra-simple but delicious meal, cook the meat or fish in the oven
together with some potatoes. Use free-range chicken, for flavour and texture.

New potatoes are a good option for the after-work cook because they
require no peeling and cook quickly. Boil them with a sprig of mint and
serve with melting butter or, as an alternative, bake them in their skins,
shiny with olive oil, and add soy sauce or balsamic vinegar towards the
end of cooking for extra-appetising colour and flavour. Any leftovers are
good for a lunchtime or supper salad with other vegetables and some
crumbled bacon.

Serves any number

chicken quarters : 1 per person
or
fish fillets or steaks : 1 per person
(weight varies according to
fish, but roughly 150-170g
of filleted fish)
new potatoes : 200-250g per person
olive oil : ½-1 tablespoon per person (a
little more if cooking chicken)
butter : small knob per person (if
cooking fish)
lemon juice : a squeeze (if cooking fish)

soy sauce : ½ tablespoon per person

or

balsamic vinegar : 1 tablespoon per person

1   Preheat the oven to 190°C fan oven/200°C or 400°F electric oven/Gas 6.

2   **If cooking the chicken** put the quarters on a baking tray. Season with salt and pepper and pour over a little olive oil. Put in the oven for 30-40 minutes (breast quarters), 40-50 minutes (leg quarters), or until the juices run clear when you stick a knife into the thickest part.

3   Wash the potatoes and cut out any blemishes. Put them in a single layer in an ovenproof dish and toss in the olive oil. Season with salt and pepper (just a little salt if you are going to add soy sauce). Put in the oven to cook for 30-50 minutes or until patched with brown and almost tender inside (the timing will depend on how many you are cooking and how much else there is in the oven).

4   **If cooking the fish,** put it in a buttered ovenproof dish. Dab with more butter and squeeze over some lemon juice. Season with salt and pepper. Cover the dish tightly with foil and cook for 10-15 minutes or until the fish is cooked all the way through.

5   When the potatoes are patched with brown, pour over the soy sauce or balsamic vinegar and turn the potatoes over in the juices. Cook for another 10-15 minutes. Roll the potatoes round in the brown juices and serve with the chicken or fish and a dressed green salad or a saucy vegetable, such as the Tuscan beans (see page 44).

COMMENTS

Mum: Excellent. The potatoes would be good with roasts or for supper. Used loose new potatoes which needed careful cleaning but it would be very convenient made with potatoes from a packet.

Rachel: Had with roast chicken. We thought the potatoes and balsamic vinegar an excellent and interesting combination.

Liz: Couldn't imagine what these potatoes would be like but they were good. I crowded them into a pyrex dish rather than on a baking tray and they took longer to cook. Used balsamic vinegar on the potatoes and in the dressing for a salad which tied the meal together nicely.

Fish Wrapped in Bacon

You can use salmon or cod fillet for this dish.

Serves any number

cod or salmon fillet : about 150g per person
mango chutney (optional) : 1 teaspoon per person
streaky bacon : 2 slices per person

1   Preheat the oven to 220°C fan oven/230°C or 450°F electric oven/Gas 8.
2   If using, spread the mango chutney on the fish. Put the bacon over the top of the fish, leaving the ends overhanging, not tucked under, so they cook properly. Season with black pepper.
3   Put in the oven for 10-15 minutes or until the overhanging ends of the bacon start to brown and the fish is cooked through.
4   Serve with baked new potatoes and spinach.

COMMENTS

Liz: Brilliant and very quick to make. At first I thought the mango chutney sounded a bit strange but I tried it and it works by adding a bit of sweetness to the dish. Used the back bacon I had in the fridge which worked fine but streaky would be better.

Mum: Used cod and mango chutney. Try not to get too thick
a portion so it can cook quickly. Tasty. Needs the spinach for colour
and sappiness or you could use another vegetable with a sauce.
Patti: The mango chutney sounded highly dubious but it
was great and the recipe is very quick and easy. Popular with
daughter, Iona (two and a half years old).

Tuscan Beans

A very easy and fragrant dish that goes well with plainly cooked meat
such as pork or lamb chops, sausages, roast chicken, fish steaks or anything that needs a bit of sauce. A good substantial dish for vegetarians
with some goat's cheese crumbled into it. Any leftovers are delicious for
lunch or supper the next day.

Feeds six as a side dish

red onion : 1
garlic : 1 clove
olive oil : 4 tablespoons
tinned chopped tomatoes : 1 x 400g tin
or
fresh tomatoes : 8
tinned haricot
or flageolet beans : 2 x 400g tin
rosemary : 1 sprig

1   Chop the red onion and crush the garlic. Fry gently in the olive oil for 5
minutes. This amount of oil adds an important richness to the dish.

2　If using fresh tomatoes, put them in a bowl and pour over boiling water. Leave for 30 seconds and drain. Peel and chop.

3　Drain the beans, rinse them and add to the pot with the chopped fresh or tinned tomatoes and rosemary. Heat through for 5 minutes, stirring occasionally so they do not stick to the pan.

4　Season with plenty of salt and pepper and remove the rosemary just before serving.

COMMENTS

Emily: The guests raved and two people took the recipe down.
Used fresh tomatoes and doubled the quantities for 11 people.
Needed plenty of rock salt. Tasted even better the next day.
I would never have thought to use that amount of oil, but it
made it. You could add a bay leaf, but not necessary.

Tarted-up Curries with Fool-proof Rice

The tastiest ready-meals are usually the curries because their flavours improve on the shelf, in the same way a chilli or home-made curry tastes better the day after you make it.

One packet generally feeds one greedy person. To make your guests feel treated rather than cheated, put a little effort into presentation and give people a choice of curries and lots of bits and pieces like naan bread and chutneys. You could also have bowls of almonds, raisins and sliced bananas if you really want to go to town.

After much experimentation, I find cooking rice in the oven the easiest, most foolproof method when you are under pressure. Basmati is less likely to stick than other long-grained rice and has a lovely perfumed-earth aroma. Serve the curries to the side of the rice rather than on top so the basmati fragrance rises off the plate.

The basic rule for quantities is 60-80g rice per person cooked in double its weight in millilitres of water. It is, conveniently enough, double its volume as well, so you can measure both the rice and the water in a measuring jug.

Serves four

2 types of ready-meal curries :	2 packets of each
basmati rice :	300g/300ml
butter :	½ tablespoon
naan bread :	4
perking-up ingredients (see 6, below) :	2
plain yoghurt :	small pot/150g
2 types of chutneys :	a pot of each

1   When you get back from work, turn the oven on to 180°C fan oven/190°C or 375°F electric oven/Gas 5.

2   Read the packet instructions on the ready-meals so you know when to put them in the oven. If they require different temperatures, you should use the higher one and put the other one in for slightly less time.

3   Put the basmati rice in a generously buttered casserole dish. Do not add salt to the rice as ready-meal curries tend to be very salty.

4   Just after your guests arrive, pour 600ml boiling water over the rice and put a lid on the pot.

5   Put the rice in the oven for 30 minutes and the curries for as long as they need. Put the *naan* bread in the oven to warm up at the end. Check that both curries are piping hot and cook for longer if necessary. Fork up the rice and leave the lid on to keep warm.

6   You can perk up the curries at the end by giving them a bit of colour, tex-

ture and freshness. Do one or more of the following to each one: stir in some roughly chopped watercress, rocket or coriander leaves; squeeze in lime juice; spoon over some yoghurt; scatter over crisply fried (but not burnt) sliced shallots or onions; add some cashews or toasted flaked almonds.

7   Serve the curries, rice, *naan* bread, yoghurt and two kinds of chutney for people to help themselves. Afterwards, offer tropical fruit and an exotic ice-cream such as coconut or ginger.

COMMENTS

Helen: 'Fluffy' rice: now I know what the bastards mean. Rice is no longer a four-letter word: a eureka experience! It is important to butter the dish. Bumping-up curries makes all the difference between a stuff-it-in-the-oven-can't-be-bothered affair and a proper meal. Whether you admit to the cheat is up to your moral fibre. Added a mixture of chopped coriander, rocket and watercress, scattered crispy fried shallots on the top, which looked good and put lime quarters and all the other businesses out to make a nice tableful.

Liz: A quick *raita* is good with this, made by mixing grated cucumber into natural yoghurt seasoned with salt and pepper.

Katherine: Works well. Used chopped-up cucumber and peppers.

Amaretti Biscuits and Compote

Rich, tasty and very quick. One tester, Frances, suggested putting it in individual glass dishes for a dinner party to show off the layered effect.

Serves six to eight

compote : 1 x 600g jar
crème fraîche : 1 big tub/500ml
caster sugar : 3 tablespoons
sherry or other booze : ½ small wine glass/50 ml
amaretti biscuits : 100g

1   Pour the compote into a serving dish. Bonne Maman is a good, widely available brand generally found near the jams or tinned fruits in delis and supermarkets. Apricot is a good flavour for this pudding. If unavailable, whizz up three tins of drained apricots with sugar to taste. M&S carton compote is also recommended.

2   Using a fork, mix together the *crème fraîche* with the sugar and sherry in a bowl. If you want to use another kind of booze, use the same quantity of fortified wines such as ginger wine or Marsala or less of a stronger liqueur e.g. 2 tablespoons brandy or Italian Amaretto.

3   Put the boozy cream on top of the compote.

4   Cover the pudding with amaretti biscuits, and keep in the fridge until ready to serve.

COMMENTS

Emily: One guest had fourths.
Helen: Put a bowl of amaretti biscuits on the table for guests
to add more with second helpings.

Frances: Used Captain Morgan dark rum for the booze which had a lovely flavour. The biscuits were nicest when they had had a few hours to soften in the mixture. Everyone found this an extremely delicious pudding. It kept well in the fridge for a few days – I just added fresh biscuits a few hours before serving.

Belinda: Instead of the compote used dried apricots, poached briefly in a light syrup and then half-liquidised. More taste, though slightly heavier than Bonne Maman. Used cocoa amaretti which were nice. *Very* quick to make.

Tarting-up Ice-cream

Ice-cream is a fail-proof pud and mid-week etiquette means nobody minds if you serve it straight from the tub. Buy more than one kind for a treat and offer fruit as an alternative.

These are ideas for adding a little extra to your ice.

Quick Date or Prune Jam

If you can find them, Medjool dates have an almost fudgy taste. Ready-to-eat prunes are a long way from the school dinner horrors of yore. The squeamish may want to think of them as 'sun-dried plums'.

Serves three to four

ready-to-eat prunes or dates : 8

orange : 1

honey : 1 tablespoon

1 Stone the dates or prunes, if necessary, and chop them up roughly.
2 Put in a pan with the juice of the orange and the honey. Cook over a low heat for a couple of minutes, stirring occasionally until thick and jammy.
3 Serve hot or cold with vanilla or chocolate ice-cream.

COMMENTS

Liz: Good. It's amazing how the prunes soak up the juice.
I added some orange zest as well. It doesn't look much in the pan
but it goes a long way because it is so concentrated.

Toasted Nuts

Toasting nuts really improves their flavour but take care they do not burn and become bitter. To serve six, put 100g flaked almonds, pecan nuts or skinned hazelnuts into a preheated oven at 190°C fan oven/200°C or 400°F electric oven/Gas 6. Bake for a few minutes until lightly browned. Watch they do not burn. Scatter the nuts over the ice-cream on its own or with the boozy vine fruits below.

Boozy Vine Fruits

Plump up raisins or sultanas with booze and put on ice-cream. I adore the combination of bourbon whisky and vanilla ice-cream but you could use many different flavour combinations.

Serves six

raisins or sultanas : 6 tablespoons/100g
bourbon or other booze : 1 small wine glass/100ml

1 Put the raisins or sultanas in a small pan. Pour over the booze.
2 Bring to the boil. Turn the heat off, and leave to infuse for an hour.

COMMENTS

Becca: Used brandy and a bit of strong coffee.
Ate it when we got back from a freezing cold walk with friends.
It made ice-cream perfect for a cold day.

Mascarpone and Berry Fool

Fools are the simplest of puddings to make in a rush and can be jazzed up with elegant biscuits like *langues de chat*, Florentines, ginger snaps and shortbread.

One of the simplest M&S cheaty recipes is to mix together a carton of their ready-made custard with a carton of compote. Swirl in some cream and Crème de Cassis at the end.

Mascarpone is an Italian cream cheese that has a luscious smooth richness. Berry mixtures can be kept in the freezer and defrosted in a couple of hours or while you are at work.

Serves six

**berry mixture
(frozen are convenient)** : 500g
mascarpone : 500g
caster sugar : 4 tablespoons

1 Let the berry mixture defrost during the day or over 2½ hours.

2   Mix the mascarpone with the caster sugar. Stir in the berries. Keep in the fridge until ready to serve.

3   Serve with smart biscuits.

COMMENTS

Clare: Really lovely. Needs something crunchy with it like biscuits. Good if somebody wants you to bring a pudding and you have to buy the ingredients on the way.
Trisha: Looks wonderfully colourful. Very delicious. Used a mixture of redcurrants and blackcurrants that were picked from the garden and frozen. Good with sharp fruit as the mascarpone is very rich.

Cheese and Fruit

The easiest way to end a mid-week meal is simply to put a platter of cheese and fruit on the table. They look wonderful served together as the colours, textures and shapes set each other off. To get away with such simplicity, you need to buy the best cheese you can get your hands on; think a bit about the combination of flavours and restrict the selection as this looks more stylish than a great mix-up. Salad leaves and raw vegetables are also good partners for cheese.

My local cheese shop owner, Patricia Michelson of the excellent La Fromagerie in Highbury (0171 359 7440), steers me through which cheeses are at their very best at a particular time of year. Here are some combinations she recommends:

Spring

Goat's cheese and crudités, fresh herbs or rocket.

Harder cheeses like Comté, Caerphilly and Cheddar with apples or pears.

Triple-cream cheeses like Explorateur with celery or radishes.

Summer

Cream cheese mixed with a little rock salt, black pepper, chopped chives and tarragon served with sourdough bread.

Tart, fresh goat's cheeses with cherries.

Denser goat's cheeses with peaches, apricots or greengages.

Strawberries and *crème fraîche*.

Alpine cheeses like Beaufort with grapes, pears or dried fruit and toasted walnuts.

Autumn

Brie with grapes (perfumed muscat grapes are very good).

Lancashire and other hard British cheeses with apples.

Gorgonzola and pears.

Winter

Stilton and other blue cheeses with pears.

Vacherin with almonds.

MENU:

Uninterrupted Gossip with Friends

WILD MUSHROOM RISOTTO
GREEK YOGHURT WITH PECAN NUTS,
BLUEBERRIES AND MAPLE SYRUP

Serves four friends

SUPPER WITH FRIENDS means attending to gossip, moans and jokes rather than pans and sauces. Even if everyone is plonked down in the kitchen, it is hard to talk properly and cook. How can you do something as mundane as turning the oven off when a friend is divulging the latest trauma/triumph in his or her love life? Most of this menu can be thrown together quickly before your friends arrive and move into wine and news.

Wild Mushroom Risotto

Oven risottos are less time-consuming than constantly stirring a pot on a hob and ideal if you want to leave the food in the oven and concentrate on the crucial details of the gossip. This uses an instant stock using soy sauce and the mushroom soaking liquid but you can use chicken stock instead if you have it.

Serves four

dried wild mushrooms :	20g
soy sauce :	1 tablespoon
mushrooms, large or button :	140g
onion :	1
butter :	large knob/30g
risotto rice (arborio or other short-grain) :	250g
flat-leaf parsley :	2 tablespoons chopped
lemon :	½

1   Preheat the oven to 190°C fan oven/200°C or 400°F electric oven/Gas 6. Pour 900ml warm water into a bowl. Add the dried wild mushrooms and soy sauce and leave to soak for 10 minutes.

2   Meanwhile, wash the fresh mushrooms and cut into bite-sized pieces. Slice the onion.

3   Melt the butter in a casserole dish. Sweat the onion in the butter over a medium heat for about 4 minutes or until softened. Add the risotto rice and stir for another minute. Season with salt and black pepper.

4   Add the dried and fresh mushrooms and the strained soaking liquid. Cover with a lid. Put in the oven for 40 minutes.

5   Roughly chop a large handful of flat-leaf parsley to get about 2 table-spoons. Squeeze the half lemon.

6   Stir the parsley and lemon juice into the risotto. Check the seasoning. Serve immediately or keep warm in the oven until ready to eat. Put a hunk of Parmesan on the table with a grater so people can add their own. Because this is a rich dish, it is best served with a salad that has a sharp vinaigrette.

COMMENTS

Monica: A really easy method which I now use regularly.
The parsley at the end adds freshness.
Mum: Very simple. Needs plenty of salt and the lemon
to sharpen up the flavour.
Aidan and Jenny: A very 'meaty' dish for vegetarians because
it is substantial and fully flavoured. A satisfying dish
on a winter's night.

Greek Yoghurt with Pecan Nuts, Blueberries and Maple Syrup

This is easily multiplied for a dinner party, or divided for a treat for one or two.

Serves four

pecan nuts : 2 handfuls/about 60g
Greek yoghurt : 400g
blueberries : 400g
maple syrup : 4 tablespoons

1   Toasting the pecan nuts makes them taste extra good. To do this, put them in a tray in the oven alongside the risotto for a couple of minutes or in a frying pan, without oil or butter, and cook over a low heat for a couple of minutes, until they just start to brown on one side. Take care they do not burn and become bitter.

2   Put the yoghurt in four bowls. Scatter over the fruit and nuts. Drizzle over the maple syrup. Keep in the fridge until ready to serve.

COMMENTS

Belinda and Isa: A winner, particularly if served in pretty bowls or layered up in glass bowls or glasses so you can see all the ingredients. The pecans can be put on foil and crisped carefully under a grill.

OFFICE AND HOME LUNCHING

THE MAIN PROBLEM about lunch food, especially when eating alone, is boredom. The smell of chilled malted bread, wilting iceberg lettuce and slimy, pallid Cheddar reminds me unmistakeably of stale office tedium.

More and more people are using lunchboxes to avoid the mounting costs of buying take-away food every day and getting stuck in the boring sandwich rut. The most practical type of food to take to work will not (a) slop everywhere and (b) waft across the office putting people off their typing. Sardines are out. So is very smelly cheese, alas, unless you can weather a reputation as the office eccentric.

Good lunchbox dishes often use up vegetables from supper. Use condiments and sauces like soy, mayonnaise, Worcestershire, Tabasco, chutneys, piccalilli, ketchup and rice vinegar to revitalise leftovers, as food palls if you eat it at two meals on the trot. Cold potatoes, leeks and crumbly Cheshire cheese in a mustardy vinaigrette, is a good dish, or a rice mixed with chopped herbs, vegetables, a spoonful of pesto and a squeeze of lemon juice. Both these can be made the night before and kept in the fridge to avoid extra hurry and worry in the morning.

Leaves wilt if kept in dressing in your lunchbox during the morning, but vegetables like broccoli and leeks are improved by a vinaigrette marinade. Couscous salads, prepared the night before, travel well. Sandwiches can survive a bit of squish and are even improved if you have tomatoes soaking their juices into the bread during the morning. The Provençal sandwich *pan bagna* is actually designed to be left for a while so the olive oil and vegetable juices soak into the bread.

Little treats like a few dried pears, pecan nuts, Italian biscuits, fruit, good chocolate and cheese give a friendly fillip to your time on earth spent in an office.

A really radical option is to escape the building altogether at lunchtime. Look very businesslike as you stride out with the air of someone off to a meeting or planning to do some urgent shopping. Then find a green spot or a spare bench, open up your box and watch the world. Beans on toast and a mug of stiff tea in a caff is another option. If you are near your office, keep your head down behind a paper to avoid the beady eyes of your colleagues queuing up for a cheese sandwich to eat at their desks.

If you do have to buy a cheese sandwich, ask the server to put a scrape of Marmite on the bread to give some bite to the Cheddar. Emphasise the scrape unless you know you are dealing with someone who understands Marmite.

When you are working at home, even cooking pasta seems like too much cooking to do for lunch for one. There are three exceptions, for me: bacon butties, the hot bacon melting the butter and ketchup into the bread; scrambled eggs; or a bowl of reheated hot soup, which is a good strategy to make you relax as you are forced to eat slowly.

Otherwise it is cold food. Ham, cheese, salad and bread (as well as pots of food like houmous and taramasalata) are the lunch-hour stalwarts when you are eating to exist. Different kinds and combinations prevent boredom. Bags of salad, such as baby spinach leaves or peppery rocket, springy with vitality, can be topped with a bit of crumbled cheese or ham, strips of roasted peppers and cherry tomatoes; muffins piled up with blue cheese, mango chutney and cucumber; honey-cured ham mixed with cold new potatoes, mayo and chopped spring onions. Peanut butter is quick, spreadable energy. Saucy salads such as coleslaw and potato salad keep for a couple of days in the fridge.

This chapter includes recipes that can be put together quite quickly for friends — should you be lucky enough to still be allowed friends and company during weekdays.

Cheese and Onion Quickies

Cheese is ever on hand for lunch (or to nibble with a glass of wine when you get back from work). In a busy week, I stock up from my local cheese shop and enjoy instant treat-snacks throughout the week. Forget gold: cheese is real alchemy, turning milk into a staggering range of forms and flavours.

Cheese and onion is a classic combination that should not be confined to crisp packets. Here are some quickies using the range of onions available.

Griddled Spring Onions

Spring onions are delicious wilted on a griddle pan. Heat up the pan. Brush trimmed spring onions with oil and cook on both sides until wilted and striped with brown. Serve with cheese on toast or in a cheese salad.

Parmesan and Crispy Shallot Salad

I normally fry onions slowly over a low heat to bring out their sweetness and to stop them burning and becoming bitter. But a good trick from Indian cooking is to fry thinly sliced shallots quickly to get them brown and crispy. Stop just before they are burnt. Add the crispy onions to a dressed green salad with shavings of Parmesan.

Lazy 'Toasted' Sandwich

Rather than using a grill, put the cheese on a piece of bread and put in a hot oven for 5 minutes or so, until the bread crisps up slightly and the cheese melts. Rub the bread with a cut clove of garlic or an onion first, if you like.

Supper Leftovers Salad

Mix some cooked leeks and cut-up cooked potatoes with cubes of cheese (crumbly white cheese like Lancashire is particularly good) and a mustardy salad dressing.

Sandwich

Sliced tomato, sliced red onion and mozzarella cheese. Season with salt.

Goat's Cheese Salad with a Honey and Walnut Oil Dressing

One without onions. Goat's cheese and walnuts or walnut oil, is a classic combination for a salad, and honey further enhances the tart cheese. Put a little honey in a pan over a low heat to make it more liquid. Add a little balsamic or wine vinegar and some olive oil and a little walnut oil, if you have it. Mix with a fork. Trickle over the salad.

Utility Rolls

These roasted vegetable rolls can be thrown into a bag and lugged anywhere. They survive the commuting crush and a day at the office. I've eaten them for lunch, as a late breakfast at my desk, before a film, or in the interval at the theatre or the opera, when they stop your mind wandering from the music or plot to your rumbling tummy.

The night before, roast the vegetables, then prepare the rolls quickly the next morning. These quantities are easily multiplied if you want a more substantial picnic or are feeding more people.

Serves two

Roasted Vegetable and Tapenade Rolls

red pepper : 1
tomato : 1
shallots : 2
basil leaves : 2 large
tapenade : 2 teaspoons

Cream Cheese or Goat's Cheese and Roasted Fennel Rolls

fennel : ½ medium bulb/150g
goat's cheese
or cream cheese : about 50g
olive oil : 2 tablespoons
rolls : 4

1   Preheat the oven to 190°C fan oven/200°C or 400°F electric oven/Gas 6.

2   De-seed the red pepper and cut into quarters. Cut the tomato into four slices.

3   Cut the fronds and thin stalks off the half bulb of fennel. Cut the half downwards into three slices.

4   Put the red pepper, tomato slices, fennel slices and shallots, in their skins, in a roasting tin and drizzle over about 1½ tablespoons of the olive oil. Season with salt and pepper.

5   Put in the oven for 40 minutes, then take out and leave to cool.

6   The next morning, squeeze the shallots out of their skin (this is easier than the slightly fiddly job of peeling uncooked shallots) and roughly slice the fennel (it is awkward if you get a large piece with a chewy bit in it).

7   Slit open four rolls, keeping them 'hinged' together at one side. Trickle a little olive oil in the bread.

8   Spread the bottom of 2 of the rolls with some tapenade, adding more or less depending on strength. Fill each with 2 quarters of roasted red pepper, 1 shallot, 2 slices of tomato and a roughly torn-up basil leaf.

9   Spread the other two rolls with cream cheese or crumble in some goat's cheese. Fill with the fennel.

10 Put in a sandwich box or in a sandwich bag and then in another plastic bag (to ensure you do not get olive oil on work papers).

Soda Bread

The simplest of all breads, that needs no kneading or rising. It is best eaten hot from the oven with melting butter and a bowl of soup and cheese, or perhaps with smoked salmon and scrambled eggs for a lunch or brunch.

Buttermilk is found in some supermarkets and some health-food shops. You could substitute milk if you cannot find it, and leave out the sugar.

Serves four

self-raising flour (white or mixed with wholemeal)	:	450g
salt	:	½ teaspoon
sugar	:	½ teaspoon
olive oil	:	1 tablespoon
buttermilk	:	280ml
water	:	50ml

1   Preheat the oven to 190°C fan oven/200°C or 400°F electric oven/Gas 6. Put the flour into a large bowl (you can sift the flour through a sieve to make the end product slightly lighter).

2   Add the rest of the ingredients. Mix together with a wooden spoon and then bring it together with your hands at the end. Use one hand if you think you might have to answer the phone or open the door. You can knead it a little at this stage to get a smoother result but this is a rustic bread and looks fine slightly rough around the edges.

3   Shape into a large circle on a non-stick baking sheet. Indent a cross in the bread using the handle of your wooden spoon. This makes the finished bread easy to divide into four parts.

4   Put in the oven for 45 minutes, until the outside is crisp and brown. Serve hot or warm.

COMMENTS

Gigi: Used white flour. I didn't think it would be easy or light enough but it was brilliant. Ate with a vegetable tagine and people could push the veg onto a fork with the bread. Buttermilk was hard to find but ordered it in at local health-food shop.

Liz: Great accompaniment to a hearty soup on a cold day:
the combination makes a meal in itself, even for big appetites.
Best eaten straight from the oven. Used all-brown flour and next
time would use 3:1 brown: white to make it a bit lighter.
Ed: This was the first bread I've ever made. The bread smells great
as it cooks. I used a bit too much flour and had to add some water.
But it was amazing: it looked like a loaf of bread!

Salmon Pasta Salad and Rocket

A recipe for those eating at home with friends or family. You can
make this a bit in advance and refrigerate. Bring out of the fridge for 15
minutes before eating so it is not chilled. The large amount of olive oil in
the dressing adds flavour and gloss to the salad.

Serves four

dried pasta bows	:	300g
mange touts	:	250g
olive oil	:	4 tablespoons
skinned salmon fillet	:	600g
lemon	:	1
smoked salmon/Parma ham (optional)	:	100g
rocket/watercress	:	3 large handfuls

1   Bring a large pan of salted water to the boil. Cook the pasta until al dente
    (usually about 8-10 minutes), putting the mange touts in the same pan to
    cook with the pasta for the last 2 minutes. Drain.
2   Meanwhile, heat a little of the olive oil in a frying pan over a high heat.

Cook the salmon fillet for about 3-5 minutes on each side, depending on its thickness, or until cooked through.

3   Take the salmon out of the pan. Add the rest of the olive oil and the juice of the lemon to the pan and stir for 30 seconds to pick up all the flavours.

4   Put the drained mange touts and pasta in a serving bowl. Pour over the lemony olive oil in the pan, then toss the pasta and mange touts in the oil. Season with salt and pepper.

5   Flake the salmon roughly. Snip the smoked salmon or Parma ham into strips. Mix the salmon and smoked salmon or ham with the pasta, taking care not to break up the salmon too much.

6   Serve at room temperature with a bowl of the rocket on the side, dressed in a little olive oil if you like.

COMMENTS

Belinda: Was proud to make this at the end of December
with our own home-grown rocket (it is easy to grow from seed)!
Could substitute potato for pasta and add some shaved Parmesan
to the rocket. The fresh salmon might remain juicier if wrapped in
foil with lemon juice and butter and baked for 5-10 minutes.
Sue: Delicious. Could add some watercress to the pasta salad to
add piquancy. It is much better fresh. We had some left over
the next day and it was a bit oily.

LOVE AFTER WORK

Cooking is one of the most fundamental and charming ways of showing love. Every cup of tea, bowl of soup or gastronomic creation feeds your lover, body and soul.

The logistics of after-work romance are not easy. I wish I had servants to shuck oysters as I bathed in asses' milk. But it is more a case of sitting at a computer terminal and speeding to the supermarket in the lunch hour. It is worth cooking at home. Every cooing couple has had meals that have brought them closer together, and being at home is always going to be far more intimate than a restaurant. Besides, there are times when love will not wait until after the pudding.

If this is new love, take care that you do not leave him or her alone for too long: just long enough to admire your taste in novels but not long enough to look inside and find the doting inscription from an old love. If this is true love, make an effort to spoil and charm them. This is an evening oasis where nothing else in the world matters.

Be simple, be light (a bulging waistband is not sexy), be prepared, break boundaries and never beg for compliments: you should be able to read your lover in a hundred other ways than words.

These are all dishes you eat partially or entirely with your bare hands. Touching food is one of life's sensuous delights. Silken asparagus, yielding fruit dripping with cool juice and sweet seafood are all classic fingertip foods that are kitchen Casanovas. Peeling fruit, pulling flesh out of crab claws or winning sweet nuts from their shells make a couple linger over a meal, savouring the rewards of good food and each other's company. You can use finger bowls, napkins or lick your own or each other's fingers.

Don't forget the candles.

Tiger Prawns Dipped in Chilli Oil

Instead of dipping prawns in mayonnaise or melted butter, try the contrast of the cool, sweet flesh and hot chilli oil. Another idea on the same lines is to dip the prawns in lime juice and then crushed black peppercorns. Makes a good starter for more people.

Serves two as a starter

cooked and shelled tiger prawns : 14
chilli oil : small bowl

1 Put the prawns on a plate with a small bowl of chilli oil.
2 Both eat straight from the one plate, dipping the seafood in the chilli-hot oil.

COMMENTS

Emily: I like prawns with their tails left on as they are more decorative. A very simple dish that lets you concentrate on more compelling matters!

Poussins with Dubonnet and Orange Sauce

Eating the wings and drumsticks of such small birds soon becomes ridiculous so, half-way through, drop your forks and eat the rest in your fingers in a rudely carnivorous fashion. Not for the squeamish or a first date. You can use chicken breasts on the bone if you prefer or, if you are feeling rich, partridge. The Dubonnet and orange is a thin *jus* rather than a gravy, so serve it with something to mop it up, like mashed potato.

Serves two as a main course

poussins : 2/about 400g each
orange : ½
Dubonnet : 2 small wine glasses/200ml

1   Preheat the oven to 190°C fan oven/200°C or 400°F electric oven/Gas 6. Put the poussins in an ovenproof dish. You want there to be some room around the birds so the sauce reduces a bit. Squeeze the half orange. Pour the orange juice and Dubonnet over the poussins. Season with salt and black pepper. Put in the oven for 45 minutes.

2   Check that the birds are cooked through properly by piercing the thickest part of a drumstick. If the juices run clear, they are done. If there is a trace of pink, put back in the oven for another 5 minutes and then check again.

3   Serve a poussin, hot, warm or at room temperature, on each plate with the Dubonnet and orange sauce and something like mashed or dauphinoise potatoes (see page 94) and a green salad or spinach.

COMMENTS

Liz: Used chicken joints. Quick and easy but very impressive to serve up and a delicious combination of flavours. The meat tastes as though it has been marinated for hours. Crispy browned skin (I suppose helped by the sugar content) and the meat is served in a 'ready-made' sauce.

Helen: The sauce is tangy and the sweetness goes well with the meat and dauphinoise potatoes. Take care not to buy bigger poussins or they take over the plate. It's a very juicy dish so when eating with your fingers, wear short sleeves!

Scallops in a Tomato and Saffron Sauce

A treat dish for Truelove that is very quick to make. Skinning and chopping the tomatoes makes all the difference. Saffron is one of those spices, like vanilla, that seems expensive but a little goes a long way and it makes the sauce special.

Serves two as a main course

tomatoes :	6
white wine :	1 small wine glass/100 ml
saffron strands :	about ½ teaspoon
garlic :	1 clove
olive oil :	1 tablespoon
scallops without roe :	250g/approx. 14 medium-sized (3-4cm thick)

1   Put the tomatoes in a bowl and cover with boiling water. Leave for 3 minutes (you are part-cooking them) and then cut them in half. Pull off the skin and push out the seeds and the acidic juice surrounding them. Chop the flesh into small pieces.

2   Pour out the wine and put the saffron in it, leaving the strands to soak for a few minutes to develop the flavour and golden colour. Crush the garlic.

3   Heat the olive oil in a pan. Add the scallops and cook over a high heat for a minute. Turn over and add the garlic. Cook for another 30 seconds. Add the tomatoes, wine and saffron. Cook for 2-3 minutes more or until the scallops are cooked (the flesh has become opaque all the way through). Season with salt and pepper and more saffron, if you want.

4   Serve with potatoes or rice and a green salad or some grated courgettes stir-fried in garlicky butter.

COMMENTS

Clare: This dish persuaded someone to come and live with me –
as a flatmate. He's had baked beans ever since. Frozen scallops
give out a lot of liquid – do not add this to the sauce.

Strawberries and Raspberries Dipped in Chocolate

Biting through dark chocolate to discover the juiciness of a red berry is devilishly seductive. You can coat the whole berry in chocolate and leave to dry on greaseproof paper, although I personally find this marginally too rich for a pudding yet delicious for petits-fours.

Serves two

plain chocolate : 50g
strawberries : 150g
raspberries : 50g

1   Melt the chocolate in a bowl set over a pan of boiling water. Do not let the bottom of the bowl touch the water.

2   Wash the strawberries but do not hull. Wash the raspberries.

3   Holding each strawberry by the stalk, dip one side in the chocolate. Arrange on a plate, chocolate side up. Dip the bottom of each raspberry in chocolate and put on the plate with the hollow-side down.

4   Serve the strawberries on a shared plate to linger over together, leaving the washing up for tomorrow.

COMMENTS

Emily: As a pudding for 11, put chocolate-coated and plain fruit
on a serving dish in a ratio of 1 chocolate fruit:10 plain fruit.
Put two types of ice-cream in the middle of the plate. Tried
blueberries, raspberries, strawberries and grapes.
Blueberries were my favourite.

MENU:

Apparently Impetuous Seduction

CHAMPAGNE
ARTICHOKE HEART AND PARMESAN SALAD
PASTA WITH PARMA HAM, ROASTED RED PEPPERS,
ROCKET AND TRUFFLE OIL
ICE-CREAM AND BOOZY HOT CHOCOLATE SAUCE

Serves one canoodling couple

THIS QUICK, LUXURIOUS dinner can be thrown together with apparently insouciant ease from the contents of your fridge, freezer and storecupboard whilst drinking champagne and flirting. The secret lies in cunning advance shopping to ensure your food supplies are a notch more luxurious than usual.

Prepare the starter, pasta ingredients and chocolate sauce before your intended arrives. Settle them down in a chair with a glass of champagne and then serve the salad. Cook the pasta and serve immediately and then reheat the sauce for the ice-cream. Three, two, one: we have lift-off!

Artichoke Heart and Parmesan Salad

A combination of up-market storecupboard and fridge classics.

Serves two as a starter

artichoke hearts (bottled or tinned)	280g
sherry vinegar or wine vinegar	few drops
olive oil (optional)	few drops
Parmesan	small hunk

1 Cut the artichoke hearts into halves. Arrange on two plates.
2 Sprinkle a few drops of sherry vinegar or wine vinegar on to the artichokes and a little of the oil that the artichokes were stored in. If they were stored in brine, use olive oil.
3 Using a knife or a potato peeler, pare about 8 shavings of Parmesan on to each plate. Season with black pepper.

COMMENTS

Diana: Having no artichokes, and finding none in the mini-market near the cinema, I raided fridge and storecupboards and produced tomato and mozzarella salad with an anchovy and parsley vinaigrette as a starter. A great success – took us to the sea and summer.

Pasta with Parma Ham, Roasted Red Peppers, Rocket and Truffle Oil

A no-cook, effortlessly luxurious sauce to go on pasta. Truffle oil is outrageously expensive but just a few drops are potent with a dangerously sexy, almost feral, aroma. This elixir of seduction transforms pasta and vamps up the meekest salad. Sprinkle on cooked food or salads but do not heat as it loses its subtle power. Its aroma also fades over time so do not hoard it in a cupboard.

Serves two as a main course

linguine or tagliatelle	:	150g
Parma ham	:	4 slices/60g
roasted red peppers		
(bottled or tinned)	:	2 tablespoons
rocket	:	handful
lemon juice	:	good squeeze
truffle oil		
(optional but exciting)	:	1 tablespoon

1   Put linguine into the boiling water and cook for 6-8 minutes, or until it is al dente.

2   Meanwhile, cut the Parma ham into strips.

3   Drain the pasta. Put in a bowl and add the roasted red pepper strips, rocket and a squeeze of lemon juice.

4   If you have it, add the truffle oil, or otherwise use oil from the pepper jar or good-quality olive oil. Season with salt and pepper. Toss and serve immediately. Put the strips of Parma ham on top of each plateful after serving the pasta, to ensure you both get equal amounts.

COMMENTS

Diana: After a 3-hour movie and half-way through pregnancy
(so I'm not looking my best), I needed a dinner which was not
only quick but extremely potent in its seductive qualities.
The sexiness of this dish lies in its simplicity, in the enhancement
of the separate parts by the sensuously luxurious truffle oil and the
lemon juice (don't underestimate the importance of the lemon –
it makes everything sing). The *prosciutto* tastes meatier, the peppers
more 'grown-up' with this dousing of earthy, masculine oil.
Anyone who isn't seduced by it frankly isn't worth seducing.
You need to share out the *prosciutto*: rowing about fair
distribution is not conducive to seduction.
Fresci: This reminded me of warm summer nights on the
Mediterranean. I loved the colours, the red and the green and
the ham. Used Spanish roasted red peppers from a tin which
were good. Very quick to make: I came down from my bath,
chopped a few things and it was cooked.

Ice-Cream and Boozy Hot Chocolate Sauce

Serve the sauce piping hot to make this dish thrilling.

Serves two

plain chocolate : 50g
milk : 2 tablespoons
Cointreau or other liqueur : 2 tablespoons
vanilla ice-cream : according to greed

1   Break the chocolate into squares, and put with the milk and Cointreau (or whatever liqueur you want to use) into a mixing bowl that fits above a pan of simmering water, without touching the water. Heat over the water for a couple of minutes, stirring occasionally until the ingredients melt. Or melt in a microwave (see Diana's tester note below).

2   Leave until just before serving. To reheat, give it a quick blast in the microwave or bring the water back to the boil and stir the sauce until it is hot.

3   Serve the ice-cream in bowls with the sauce on top.

COMMENTS

Diana: How difficult this pudding was. Not because it's a hard recipe but because once you'd been given the idea of a simple chocolate sauce with the addition of liqueur, where could things end? Cointreau, that walnut liqueur bought on holidays in Italy, *crème de framboises*, Amaretti . . . Eventually I made one with Cointreau and added raw sliced oranges, and the other with the addition of a hefty 3 tablespoons of raspberry liqueur. If I could have found fresh raspberries on a cold January night, I would have broken the cardinal rule about being seasonal and enjoyed a very early taste of summer. I stuck the sauce ingredients in the microwave for 40 seconds. You'll panic if you do this, because the mixture does separate and go lumpy. Just give it a good beating with a wooden spoon till it all amalgamates and becomes glossy. Then just give the sauce another blast of heat before serving.

Helen: Used brandy. Put the sauce directly on to vanilla ice-cream and it is, like the Southern belle said: 'Jus' like ah daahed and gahn to heaven!'

HEALTH KICK

The recipes in this chapter are for those days when you want something light, perhaps in the summer or on a Monday evening after a weekend of filling food.

The British diet has been greatly improved by the influence of the healthy cuisines of other countries. Pasta and stir-fries, low in fat and high in veg, are now commonplace. Pulses and beans are recovering from their dull, farty reputation as food fashions swing south and east to such dishes as Indian *dhals*, Spanish chickpea stews and Moroccan *tagines* served on couscous. Be it Thai fragrant spiciness or Provençal gusto, ripe fruit or the many different textures and tastes of vegetables, healthy eating has come a long way from earnest brown stodge.

Colourful food, bright as traffic lights, has always seemed to me very appealing (roasted beetroot on dark green spinach leaves; blushing peaches and crimson cherries; bold carrots and glowing oranges) so it is interesting that green and red/orange vegetables are thought by nutritionists to be particularly good for you.

For 'health kick' do not read 'diet'. Dieting is a late twentieth-century neurosis that leaves you with too little petrol in your tank to think vigorously and enjoy life. It is pretty normal to moan occasionally about your weight because a bit of padding is a by-product of a seden-tary lifestyle. And of course it is unhealthy to be seriously overweight. But many women (far, far, far too many: most of us, in fact) expend an unnecessary amount of angst and energy worrying about the 'awful' unorthodoxies of our bodies. I partly put this down to dieting itself, which makes your brain feel as weak and depleted as the rest of your body and further erodes your self-esteem.

We all want to feel our best but what exactly is this? Having a healthy zoom to your life is completely different to self-denial and self-disgust. The message is getting through that the common-sense (if boringly undramatic) answer to weight-loss and maintenance is to eat reasonably healthily, as a long-term habit rather than a drastic measure, and lead a moderately active life. Your weight gradually settles naturally at what it is meant to be. This is not the body of a 16-year-old. Perhaps part of the reason for recidivist, unnecessary dieting is a doomed yearning for youth.

There are degrees of weight-worry, from the minor moans to eating disorders, but there is no denying that it is endemic in our society (for some men as well as many women). This is something to be challenged whenever it gets to the stage that your relationship with food is basically one of guilt and self-consciousness instead of energy and pleasure.

As for how men see women, I think they are mostly more into swoop-ing curves and vitality than identikit sets of jangling bones. Lady, wear your curves!

Provençal Bean Salad

This deliciously fragrant salad can be turned into a first course or light lunch by crumbling in some goat's cheese.

Serves six as a side dish, four as a starter

French beans	:	250g
garlic	:	¼ clove
basil leaves	:	6
olive oil	:	2 tablespoons
tinned kidney beans	:	1 x 420g tin

1   Put a pan of water on to boil and meanwhile take the stalks off the beans (I think it is a waste of time to take the elegant, pointy 'tops' off as well). Cook the beans for 4 minutes, or until tender but still firm. Undercooked beans are a mistake: make sure they are just past the squeaky stage.

2   Crush the garlic with the blade of a knife or in a press. Tear up the basil leaves. Mix the garlic and torn-up basil leaves with the olive oil in a serving bowl.

3   Drain the green beans. Drain the kidney beans and rinse the tinning liquid off them. Mix the green and red beans together with the dressing, and season with salt.

COMMENTS

Susan: Garlic really adds interest to the kidney beans which can be a bit bland. A good alternative to goat's cheese would be shaved Parmesan. What about chicken livers?
Patti: Very delicious. I'm not fond of kidney beans but this dish was really nice. Could use borlotti beans instead.
Added some Stilton.

Chicken, Orange and Pine-nut Salad

Soak just-poached chicken in a tangy fat-free dressing to give it plenty of flavour and juiciness. Add toasted pine nuts for flavour and texture. I've also eaten this with broccoli left over from the night before, spring onions and chunks of cucumber instead of salad leaves. The chicken poaching liquid can be used as a light stock for soups or sauces.

Serves two

chicken breasts :	**2, skinned and boneless**
orange juice :	**1 small wine glass/100ml**
soy sauce :	**½ tablespoon**
pine nuts :	**4 tablespoons**
salad leaves or other greens :	**a large handful or two**

1 Put the chicken breasts in a small pan. Cover with water. Bring to the boil then turn the heat down and simmer for 15-20 minutes. Check that the chicken is cooked all the way through and there is no trace of pink inside.

2 Mix together the orange juice and soy sauce. If you like, toast the pine nuts in a dry pan for a minute or two, until they are starting to brown. Take care not to burn.

3 Take the chicken out of the poaching liquid and cut into bite-sized pieces using a knife and fork. Put in the orange and soy sauce for a few minutes so that the meat absorbs the dressing as it cools.

4 Mix the chicken with the pine nuts and salad leaves. Use the orange and soy sauce mixture as the salad dressing. Season with pepper and a little more soy sauce, if you want it to be a bit saltier.

COMMENTS

Patti: A genius recipe for dieters (I'm trying to lose post-pregnancy pounds) because it doesn't have any oil in it. I think of diet food as so dreadful and this was really good. Ate it with rocket and lamb's lettuce.
Katherine: I liked this: it was very light and very fresh. Toasted the pine nuts under the grill.

Fruit in a Ginger and Lime Syrup

Use any fruit you like. Using just one colour of fruits, red, green or yellow, say, looks nice. My suggestion for a smart, mixed-colour fruit salad would be as below. A slosh of Cointreau or rum adds some wickedness to this dish.

Serves four

ginger root : about 5 x 1cm when peeled
limes : 2
caster sugar : 2 tablespoons
mangoes : 2
bananas : 2
strawberries : 250g
blueberries : 200g

1 Peel the ginger and cut into four long strips. Juice the limes. Put 150ml water in a pan with the sugar. Heat gently until the sugar has dissolved, drawing a spoon gently over the undissolved sugar in the bottom of the pan to help it along.

2   When the sugar has dissolved, add the lime juice and ginger. Bring to the boil and boil for 3 minutes to get a sugar syrup. Leave to cool a bit.

3   As the ginger and lime syrup cools, prepare all the fruit as follows, putting everything in a serving bowl as you go. Peel the mangoes and cut into slivers off the stone. (A smarter way is to cut 'cheeks' off the mango and cut the flesh on each cheek down and across. Turn the cheek inside out so cubes of mango stick out. Run a knife or spoon close to the skin to get the cubes off. Then cut the rest of the mango off the stone.) Peel and slice the bananas. Wash, hull (pull out the stalk and any of the tasteless white core inside that comes with it) and quarter the strawberries. Wash the blueberries.

4   Pour the sugar syrup over the fruit, with the ginger.

5   Ideally, leave the fruit to marinate in the syrup for at least a couple of hours so the ginger flavour develops. Take the ginger out just before serving, making sure you have fished out all four pieces.

6   Serve the fruit salad on its own or with frozen yoghurt or ice-cream.

COMMENTS

Clare: The flavour of the ginger developed really well and tasted best of all the next day.

WEEKENDS

Saturday Night Showtime

SATURDAY NIGHT SHOWTIME

THE MOST ENJOYABLE part of cooking a dinner party is well before the meal. I love the time at around 5 or 6pm when, chopping and stirring, scheming and seasoning, you are surrounded by smells, sounds and colours. Slow-bursting caramel, the aroma of freshly ground spices or garlic in olive oil, the cool curves of peppers and pears, sugar-crunch, pan-sizzle, the liquid silks of creamy sauces, scarlet chillies and the bright shock of citrus fruits: cooking is sensory nourishment and the weekend is when you have the luxury of time to enjoy it.

By the meal, your senses have been satiated and, for the cook, the people are more interesting than the food. Most of the work for these recipes can be done before everyone arrives so you can concentrate on the food and then on the people. So no tricksy sauces and last-minute fol-de-rols.

People are less formal about entertaining than they used to be. Bring out the glamorous wedding crystal and fish knives by all means but the fundamental principle of hospitality is, after all, to make your guests happy and this can happen in many ways. What makes a dinner really special? Sparky ideas, humour, mental and emotional generosity and being happy together.

As for the food and drink, you need to push the boat out a bit for your own pleasure and sense of occasion, as well as to treat guests who have made the journey to your door. But, again, fairly simple food served with warmth is better than an overt display with no heart and a lot of fuss. The recipes in this chapter are relatively easy because anxiety goes against the spirit of the event.

Alcohol is undeniably a part of the energy of the evening. You can launch the dinner like a rocket into the night with a bottle of fizz, a cocktail or an aperitif like Dubonnet or Pineau de Charentes. Provide a good soft drink for anyone not having alcohol. I'm very fond of ginger beer with a slice of lime. Add gin for those who are boozing. It is essential to have plenty of water and water glasses on the table to quench thirst.

It is hard to predict how people will shake down together. Some people go out to encounter differences; others want cosy chats. Someone is tired or in a bad mood. Someone else has been cooped up all week and wants to talk non-stop. You can do a certain amount of orchestration, drawing in the quiet flutes by interrupting the trumpets and modulating or varying the over-played themes. In the end the evening generally does move of its own accord, mysteriously, into some kind of harmony.

Here are some initial ideas to keep the mood good. Do not invite anyone you do not like. Bringing bad vibes into your home is usually avoidable. Inviting someone you yourself do not know very well gives the evening a different impetus. Do not invite a pair of singles and put them together for the entertainment of the couples. Ruthlessly interrupt warring couples who have fallen into a private riff. Ditto anyone who is drunk and obsessing. Gently coax the guest feeling party paralysis. Beware post-mortems after one or two people have left: it makes the others feel self-conscious.

Save up a treat for the end, such as chocolates, a really good cheese or some pudding wine. It helps the evening to sail on for as long as the conversation has puff and acts as a reward for the cook who can sit back and relax now that the food is all served.

Some evenings meander enjoyably, others rise like a balloon to travel over new territory. Sometimes you feel slack, let down and exhausted; more often I lie in bed the next morning, gradually unravelling conversations and moods and thinking about how variously interesting people are and ultimately worth any amount of effort, risk — and washing up.

Goat's Cheese and Chorizo Tart

You can assemble this tart in advance and keep it in the fridge, putting it in the oven 20 minutes before you want to eat. Ready-rolled puff pastry is the really lazy option or you can roll out ready-made (one tester used a wine bottle as they didn't have a rolling pin). At the other end of the effort-scale, home-made rough puff pastry is not as laborious as you might think (although it is time-consuming) and utterly delicious. You can make up a batch to keep in the fridge for extra-special, buttery pie toppings and tart bases.

Serves six as a starter, four as a main course

ready-rolled puff pastry :	375g
leeks :	5 medium
olive oil :	1 tablespoon
goat's cheese :	100g
chorizo :	10 thin slices/about 60g

1   Preheat the oven to 190°C fan oven/200°C or 400°F electric oven/Gas 6. Put the puff pastry on a baking tray.

2   Cut the leeks into thin slices and soften in the olive oil for 5 minutes.

3   Meanwhile, cut the cheese into small pieces and the *chorizo* into quarters.

4   Put the *chorizo* over the pastry. Spread the leeks on top and dot the cheese all over the tart. You don't want the *chorizo* showing because it burns. Season with black pepper and bake for 15-20 minutes. Serve hot or warm.

COMMENTS

Helen: Cut the pastry into circles and added halved cherry tomatoes which made a good, colourful addition.

Al and Katie: Was quite a talking point at the meal. A recipe that looks as though it takes ages to make but takes no time at all.

Scallop, Parma Ham and Spinach Salad

An easy, quick salad for when you are feeling rich. Some steamed and sliced Jerusalem artichokes or some cooked new potatoes would be a good addition. You can use the pinky-orange scallop roes in this dish, if they come with the scallops, or buy them without.

Serves six as a starter, four as a main course

baby spinach : 400g
Parma ham : 100g
scallops with or without roe : 24 medium or 12 large
(over 5cm thick)
olive oil : 4 tablespoons
lemon : ½

1   Arrange the washed baby spinach on six plates. Cut up the Parma ham and scatter over the spinach.
2   If you have large scallops, cut in half, crossways, to get two thinner discs that will cook more quickly and evenly. Cook the scallops in two or three batches in a little olive oil over a high heat. Give them about a minute on each side and a little longer if necessary so the outside browns slightly and the flesh is opaque all the way through. Turn the heat off under the pan.
3   Scatter the scallops over the spinach and Parma ham.
4   Pour the olive oil and the juice of the half lemon into the frying pan and stir around to make a warm dressing. Season with salt and pepper and drizzle over the leaves, scallops and ham.

Helen: A lovely combination. You could put everything into a bowl and toss it but you would have to watch out for those guests taking too many scallops. Perfect starter because it's light, very tasty and a true appetiser that sets you off but doesn't fill you up.

Plum Chicken

Very easy to make. The chicken skin crisps nicely in the oven, while the fruit collapses into a sauce below.

Serves six

onions :	2 medium
olive oil :	2 tablespoons
plums :	about 14/1kg
ginger root :	about 4 x 2cm, when peeled
soy sauce :	1-2 tablespoons
chicken :	6 quarter portions (leg or breast)
caster sugar :	pinch
coriander (optional) :	2 tablespoons chopped

1 Preheat the oven to 190°C fan oven/200°C or 400°F electric oven/Gas 6.
2 Chop the onions and soften in a tablespoon of the olive oil over a low heat for 10 minutes. Meanwhile, cut the plums into halves or quarters to get rid of the stones. Peel the ginger and cut into very small pieces.
3 Put the plums, softened onion and ginger into a large ovenproof dish. Pour over a tablespoon of the soy sauce.

4   Put the chicken on top of the plums. Drizzle about a tablespoon of olive oil over the chicken. Season with salt and pepper. Cook for 40-50 minutes. Check that the chicken is cooked by piercing at the thickest point with a knife to check that the juices run clear.

5   Put the chicken on serving plates. Stir the plums around in the cooking dish and add more soy sauce and sugar to taste, depending on how tart or sweet the plums are. Spoon the sauce around the chicken and scatter over the chopped coriander, if using.

6   Serve with boiled, dauphinoise (see page 94) or baked potatoes and a green salad or courgettes in summer and stir-fried or steamed greens or broccoli in the winter.

COMMENTS

Nicky: Yum yum. I can imagine other sweet fruits like peaches working really well, too. Good Victorias would make it extra wonderful. Kieran found it sweet yet savoury with a real zing.

Susan: The ginger is a warming addition. Beware the use of unripe plums or the result is a little too sour-and-sweet.

Mum: Good, tangy flavour and colour.

Fresci: I love the subtly intense and unusual mixture of ginger, plum and soy.

Moroccan Spiced Lamb

Neck fillets are good for entertaining as they are quick to cook and tender to eat. This dry marinade forms a slight crust when cooked. Include the crushed insides of 3 cardamom pods, a tablespoon of crushed coriander seeds and a teaspoon of crushed cumin if you want to add another note to the spice mixture.

Serves six as a main course

ginger root : about 15cm length
coarsely ground black pepper : 6 teaspoons
ground cinnamon : large pinch
lamb neck fillets : 6/about 1.4kg

1   Ideally, prepare the dry-spice marinade the night, morning or a couple of hours before you want to eat, but you can do it just before cooking. Peel and finely grate the root ginger. Grating the root is the most arduous part of this dish because it is so fibrous. Mix with the pepper. You can buy black peppercorns ready-ground or grind your own with a mortar and pestle or in a pepper mill. Add the cinnamon and a level teaspoon of salt.

2   Spread the pepper mixture roughly over the lamb neck fillets and leave in the fridge until ready to cook.

3   Preheat the grill to high. Cook the fillets for around 6 minutes on each side or until brown on the outside but still pink in the middle. Cook for a couple of minutes longer if you like your lamb well done. You can grill the fillets before serving the first course and keep them warm in the oven.

4   Cut the lamb into chunks and divide between the plates according to appetites. Goes well with dauphinoise potatoes (see page 94) or *tabbouleh* and a green salad or spinach. The Tuscan bean recipe on page 44 would be good too.

COMMENTS

Mum: We enjoyed this very much. Hadn't used fillets before and thought they were quite a find. The number of fillets is tricky because one is too big for one person but half isn't quite enough. Go by the total weight to judge quantities.
Emily: A doddle to make and delicious. Bought the black pepper

ready-ground and used cardamom. Vital to serve something like dauphinoise potatoes to give it some sauce.

Ed: Very easy to make and good. I thought it would be too gingery, but it wasn't.

Fish Steaks with Sicilian Pepper Sauce

This recipe works with cod fillet, or swordfish or tuna steaks. I like tuna cooked through but, if you like it raw in the middle, cook the sauce separately and add the tuna 5 minutes before the end. Cut through the fish to see when it is done to your liking.

The first three stages can be done the day or morning before the dinner and kept in the fridge.

Serves six, as a main course

onions :	2
garlic :	2 cloves
olive oil :	4 tablespoons
peppers :	2 red, 2 yellow
tomatoes :	8
balsamic vinegar :	2 tablespoons
caster sugar :	2 tablespoons
capers :	2 tablespoons
tomato purée :	4 tablespoons
fish fillet steaks :	6 x 170-200g pieces

1　Slice the onions and crush the cloves of garlic. Heat up the olive oil in a casserole dish. It seems a lot but adds richness to the dish. Soften the onion and garlic in the oil over a low heat for about 10 minutes, while you de-seed the peppers and cut them into small pieces.

2   Add the peppers to the pot. Roughly chop the tomatoes and add to the pot. Add the balsamic vinegar, sugar, capers and tomato purée. Cover and simmer for 20 minutes.

3   Season the sauce with salt and pepper and add more sugar or vinegar if necessary.

4   About 10 minutes before you are ready to serve the first course, preheat the oven to 190°C fan oven/200°C or 400°F electric oven/Gas 6. Put the fish in an ovenproof dish. Wash away any blood as it can taste bitter.

5   About 5 minutes before you sit down to the first course, pour the sauce over the fish and put in the oven for 15-20 minutes or until cooked through (it will depend upon the thickness of the fish). Take care the fish does not overcook and dry out.

6   Serve the fish with the sauce, potatoes and a dressed green salad.

COMMENTS

Helen: Made it with tuna. An utter wow. It is impressively colourful:
a nice dish to put on the table. The sauce balances the texture
and the chunkiness of the tuna and the slight piquancy of
the capers is good.

Dauphinoise Potatoes

A classic dish that can sit warm in the oven until you are ready to serve. Easy to make, especially if you search through your kitchen *bric-à-brac* and find the slicing attachment to your food processor.

Dauphinoise potatoes are useful for adding a sauce to meat such as a roast or the dry-marinated Moroccan lamb recipe on page 91.

Serves 5-6

potatoes : 4-5 large/about 1.4kg
butter : 50g
garlic : 2 cloves
double cream : 1 medium pot/290ml

1   Preheat the oven to 190°C fan oven/200°C or 400°F electric oven/Gas 6. Peel the potatoes and cut into thin slices. Smear the bottom of a large ovenproof dish with some of the butter and cut the rest into small pieces. Crush the garlic.

2   Put half the potatoes into the dish. Dot with half the remaining butter and all the garlic. Season with salt and black pepper.

3   Put the rest of the potatoes on top. Dot with the rest of the butter. Season with salt and pepper. Pour over the cream. It must be double cream.

4   Cook for an hour or until the potatoes are tender and the top patched with brown. It will take longer if you have other dishes in the oven. Cover with foil if the top starts to burn but the potatoes in the centre are not ready. Serve warm or hot.

VARIATIONS

Wild Mushroom

Soak 20g dried wild mushrooms for 15 minutes and drain. Dice 70g Parma ham. Put both in the middle of the potatoes with the garlic. Goes well with chicken, game and beef.

Dill and Mustard

Dollop 3 tablespoons of Dijon mustard and plenty of chopped dill in the middle of the potatoes with the garlic. Goes well with ham, pork and fish.

Helen: This is now my impress-anybody-who-comes-round vegetable. The mushrooms and Parma ham don't overwhelm the flavours of whatever else you are serving and add texture: you have the softness of the potatoes and then some chewy flavour. I make this so often that I got a food processor for Christmas.
Ed: Less complicated than other dauphinoise recipes. Cooked the wild mushroom version which was delicious: very rich and very indulgent (and expensive). Once used single instead of double cream which was a mistake: it was thin and watery.
Went well with the Moroccan lamb.

Sweet Ricotta with Peaches and Pine Nuts

If you want to experiment you can add all sorts of sweet chunks to this dish, such as little bits of chocolate, angelica, candied peel, other fruits. Blueberries are particularly delicious as an alternative to peaches.

Serves six

pine nuts : **6 tablespoons**
peaches/nectarines : **5**
ricotta : **400g**
icing sugar : **6 tablespoons**

1 In a dry pan, lightly roast the pine nuts over a medium heat for a minute or two, taking care they do not burn and become bitter.
2 Wash the peaches or nectarines and cut into small pieces.
3 Using a fork, mix the ricotta with the icing sugar. Mix in the peaches.
4 Divide the mixture between six ramekins and sprinkle over the pine nuts. Refrigerate until you are ready for pud.

COMMENTS

Helen: A really easy, good pud. I have also made this by mixing the pine nuts into the ricotta, putting some sugar on the top and grilling it to get a crunchy top. It is nice to have a recipe that is so unpreoccupied with those terrifying itsy-bitsy ingredients one can so easily forget, or never find.

Lemon Sorbet with Apricots in a Gin and Vanilla Syrup

An unusual, fragrant and subtle pudding. Make or buy the lemon sorbet, and serve the dish with some delicate biscuits.

Serves six

apricots : 18
caster sugar : 3 tablespoons
vanilla pods : 2
or
vanilla extract : 1-1½ teaspoons to taste
gin : 3 tablespoons
lemon sorbet : 6 scoops

1   Halve and de-stone the apricots. This should be easy if they are ripe. If they do not come away easily, remove the stones once the apricots have been poached.

2   Put 300ml water in a large pan with the sugar. Add another tablespoon of sugar if the apricots are not quite ripe. Heat slowly so the sugar dissolves, gently drawing a spoon over the bottom of the pan to help it along. It takes a couple of minutes. When the sugar has dissolved, turn up the heat and boil for 3 minutes to make a sugar syrup.

3   Slit open the vanilla pods and scrape the black seeds out into the sugar syrup. They seem to get everywhere – under your fingernails, on the oven, anywhere but the pan. The handle of a teaspoon is a good tool to scoop them out. Put the pods in, too.

4   Add the apricot halves and simmer for 2-4 minutes, or until tender but not falling apart.

5   Add the gin and stir gently. Leave to cool and marinate in the liquid.

6   Serve the apricots on their own with their sauce, or with lemon sorbet and delicate biscuits.

COMMENTS

Susan: Served it with amaretti biscuits which sat on top for a bit to soak up the juices. Go gently on the vanilla. I used too much essence and as a result lost the flavour of the gin.

Joe: Used dried apricots which have a stronger taste, so the taste is more overpoweringly of apricots. Very good with the lemon sorbet.

Plums with Amaretto Mascarpone and Toasted Nuts

Boozy cream melting on to hot plums, with a crunch of toasted nuts. Amaretto is a liqueur I'm not mad about as a drink but like in puddings (and the bottle is gloriously vulgar: it looks like an outsized bottle of aftershave). You could use brandy instead.

The first five stages can be done before your guests arrive and you can quickly reheat the plums after the main course. Or prepare everything in advance and cook the plums while you are eating the starter or main course.

Serves six

ripe plums : 18
caster sugar : 4-6 tablespoons
mascarpone cheese : 250g
Amaretto liqueur/brandy : 1½ tablespoons
pecan nuts/almonds : 80g

1   Cut the plums in half. Pull out any stones that come away easily but leave the rest as they will come out more easily when the plums are cooked. Put the plums, cut-side-up, in an ovenproof dish. Sprinkle the sugar over them, using more or less depending on the sweetness of the plums.

2   Mix together the mascarpone and liqueur in a small serving bowl. Refrigerate until ready to serve.

3   Toast the pecan nuts or almonds in a dry frying pan for a minute or so, until they are just turning light brown, but take care they do not burn and become bitter.

4   Put the plums in an oven that has been preheated to 190°C fan oven/200°C or 400°F electric oven/Gas 6. Cook for 10-15 minutes, or until the fruit is giving and juicy.

5   Take any of the stones out that are left in the plums. Scatter the toasted pecans on top.

6   Put the hot plums, the cold Amaretto mascarpone and a bowl of sugar on the table for guests to help themselves, or dollop the mascarpone on top of the plums and bring to the table.

COMMENTS

Helen: Very easy, and the toasted nuts are fantastic.
Put mascarpone on table for people so they can help themselves
to more with seconds. It's a good tip that you can cook the plums
and then remove the stones. Many a plum has been decimated
as I've tried to wrestle with the stone and you are lucky to
get away with all your fingers at the end.
Susan: If your local shop, like mine, has never even heard of mascarpone,
a good substitute is thick cream whipped with cream cheese.
Sue: We had some of the cream mixture left over to use with mince pies.
The plums were very good cold the next day.

Creamy Rice Pudding

This is a slow way to make rice pud, designed so the rice gradually melts to softness and you get a nice caramelised skin. Cook something else in the oven like a stew or some baked potatoes to make use of the heat. I've also cooked this rice pudding at a slightly higher temperature (150°C fan oven/160°C or 325°F electric oven/Gas 3) with the mulled lamb recipe in The Dragon to Dinner menu (see page 32). It took 2 hours.

For variation, you can add other flavourings such as the crushed insides of 3 cardamom pods and the grated rind of half an orange or some cinnamon.

Any left over pudding rice can be used in a risotto. It is not as smart as other short-grained rices like arborio but works perfectly fine for a mid-week supper dish. Vanilla extract is more fragrant and less synthetic than vanilla essence.

Serves five to six

pudding rice : 100g
caster sugar : 4 tablespoons
full-fat milk : 750ml/1½ pints
double cream : medium pot/290ml
vanilla extract/essence : ½ teaspoon
nutmeg : a few gratings

1 Preheat the oven to 140°C fan oven/150°C or 300°F electric oven/Gas 2.
2 Mix the rice, sugar, milk, cream and vanilla together in an ovenproof dish. Do not worry about the small amount of rice: it swells as it absorbs the milk and cream. Grate enough nutmeg to lightly dust the surface of the pudding.
3 Put the dish on a baking tray, to prevent any spillage mess if your dish is full of liquid, and put in the oven. Cook for about 2½-3 hours. The surface will have a tasty, caramel-coloured skin that bubbles up as it cooks.
4 Serve warm on its own, or with compote, stewed fruit or jam.

COMMENTS

Monica: Yummy. Added cardamom.
Susan: We ate it with *dulce de leche*, as we used to when living in Argentina, which makes it extra-rich. If you cannot get hold of it, you can put a tin of condensed milk in a pan, cover with water and boil for an hour. Let it cool slightly before opening the tin and dollop the thick, fudgy sauce on the pud.

MENU:

Back to the Seventies Dinner

VODKA AND ORANGE AND CHEESY PINEAPPLE BITS
PRAWN COCKTAIL IN AVOCADO PEARS
DUCK WITH FENNEL AND ORANGE
PEACH MELBA

Serves six groovers

ARE THE SEVENTIES 'In' or 'Out'? Hey, who cares? These dishes are simply good to eat. Deck out in flares, June-blue eye shadow, lapels down to Australia, spangles, jangles and stars, put some funky vibes on the hi-fi and get down to a seventies retro-chic dinner of dishes which you secretly wish had never gone out of fashion.

When your guests have eased their flares and false eyelashes through the front door, give them a pre-health-conscious quantity of vodka and orange before dinner, this time around with good-quality orange juice and slices of lime, and cheesy-pineapple bits stuck on cocktail sticks in a half grapefruit. Cheesy's the word, but still good. Engineer a surprise power-cut, after the cooking, as a bonus seventies event.

Prawn Cocktail in Avocado Pears

This has never gone out of fashion according to my taste buds. Other people have confessed to me that they sometimes sneak a pot of it into their supermarket basket, so I am not alone. You can use shop-bought prawn cocktail or quickly make your own. Small North Atlantic prawns are sweeter and tastier than large tiger prawns from warm waters.

Serves six as a starter

mayonnaise : 6 tablespoons
tomato purée : 3 level teaspoons
Worcestershire sauce : few shakes
cooked small prawns : 300g
avocados : 3

1 Mix the mayonnaise with the tomato purée, a few shakes of Worcestershire sauce and some black pepper. Mix with the cooked prawns and refrigerate.

2 Cut the avocados in half and take out the stones. Put on plates, one half per person, and fill with prawn cocktail, putting any extra on the side of the plate.

3 Serve with lemon wedges, or lemon slices if you want to be retro.

Alex: I'd forgotten how good small prawns were. Couldn't find Worcestershire sauce in Brussels so used lots of lemon and some soy sauce instead. Good with a Portuguese white wine from the Douro.

Al: This has been our family Boxing Day starter since about 1972 and I feel slightly gloomy eating it at other times because it has the feeling that Christmas is over.

Duck with Fennel and Orange

A quick updated variation on the duck *à l'orange* combination. If you want to make it more special, add some slices of fresh orange to the sauce and wrap some bacon round the outside of the duck breasts before browning them.

If you like, use curly or flat leaf parsley to add colour and flavour but chop it finely: one of the sins of the seventies was to have inedible sprigs of tickly parsley left whole on the plate as a 'garnish'.

You can cook this just before your guests arrive, or further in advance, and reheat before serving.

Serves six as a main course

duck breasts :	6
oranges (optional) :	3
parsley (optional) :	2 tablespoons chopped
olive oil :	1 tablespoon
fennel :	2 bulbs
spring onions :	5
orange juice :	420ml
soy sauce :	1 tablespoon

1   If you are using the orange and parsley, prepare them right at the beginning. Peel the orange and cut out the segments by sawing the fruit out from between the pith. Finely chop the parsley.

2   Take the skin off the duck breasts. Brown the meat in the oil in a large casserole dish over a high heat.

3   Meanwhile, cut the fennel into small chunks and the spring onions into 5cm lengths.

4   Add the orange juice, soy sauce, fennel and spring onions to the duck in the casserole, and mix. Turn down the heat to medium and cook for 7-10 minutes, turning the meat over once or twice until it is cooked but still pinkish and the sauce has reduced down to a slightly sticky consistency. Season with salt and pepper.

5   Reheat just before serving. If using, add the orange segments near the end, so they just heat through, and the parsley at the last minute.

6   To be really retro, serve with onion rings and potato croquettes (home-made or cooked from frozen) and some sort of greenery like broccoli, spinach or a green salad. Onion rings are naughtily nice and not to be missed but, with the benefit of hindsight, I prefer new potatoes, cooked with a sprig of mint and glossy with melting butter, to the brown rounds of potato croquettes.

COMMENTS

Anil and Alice: Cooked this as a supper dish for two and wrapped the duck in bacon, browned it and then added the rest of the ingredients. Tangy and delicious (Alice is not normally a fan of duck *à l'orange*).

Isa and Mark: Would be good to lay fresh orange slices over the duck when finished.

Peach Melba

A classic.

Serves six

raspberries (fresh or defrosted) : 500g
caster sugar : 2-4 tablespoons
peaches : 6
vanilla ice-cream : 6 scoops

1   Whizz up the raspberries in a food processor. Add more sugar if you like sweet sauces, or leave less for a sharper sauce that is a contrast to the ice-cream. I personally do not sieve out the pips but very polite people, who do not like sticking their fingers in their mouth at the table, can find them troublesome.

2   Cut the peaches in half and twist out the stones.

3   Put two peach halves on each plate. Put a small scoop of vanilla ice-cream on each half and pour around the raspberry sauce.

COMMENTS

Helen: Fab. Definitely on the dinner party easy puddings list. Used nectarines. I had a vision of smashing meringues with a mallet and scattering them over the top. We had a debate on whether to sieve out the pips and decided it was better not to, to give some texture and more oral gratification, especially for those who had given up smoking (it was a January dinner).

TREATS FOR TWO

COOKING FOR TWO *is* a treat compared to feeding a family or lots of people. Far less work, shopping, cooking and clearing up. Far more time to talk. You can splash out on wonderful ingredients and a really special bottle of wine without breaking the bank. You can make all sorts of sauces and use techniques that are impossible for larger numbers. Time and place are flexible. Eat outside, inside, reclining on a sofa, stretched out on the floor, brunch at 3pm in your dressing gown, supper at 6pm before a long bath and bed, supper in bed even (but toast at your peril). Time expands at the weekend. Rules bend and schedules melt.

What can be more spoiling for a friend than turning up at their house with supper and a bottle of wine? Or going out to the shops, leaving your beloved in bed or deep in a book, and coming back with riches to consume and the Sunday papers? Food is the ultimate consumer pastime, the any-day retail therapy.

We all have our own ideas of what makes a treat. The most obvious are the luxuriously expensive foods that you can only afford to eat occasionally. Lobster, crayfish and langoustines seem all the more delicious for being so dear and the anticipation mounts because they take so long to disrobe. Actually eating shellfish is simplicity itself: a blob of mayonnaise or a squeeze of lemon on the sweet flesh. The finest steak, scallops and grouse are similar treats that are best prepared without fuss.

Then there are the foods that are specially seasonal such as freshly picked peas from someone's garden or English asparagus and strawberries. Or foods that are rare because they just come from one place. Tracking down top-class foods satisfies the hunter-gatherer instinct. Discover a delicious ham, a really good Cheddar or smoked salmon. Craft-made products like these vary as much as wines in taste and it is fun to try different kinds.

For more local hunter-gathering, the weekend is the time when you might go out of your way to go to a specialist food shop and buy a really good cut of meat, a perfectly ripe cheese that oozes over the plate, some fragrant olives or fish that is sparklingly fresh off a fishmonger's slab.

But a treat can also be found round the corner. It may be a piggy indulgence, like chip butties and cream on Frosties. Anything that you were not allowed as a child (Ribena does it for me), or anything that you ate often as a child but not often nowadays (fish fingers, spaghetti hoops). Then there are the other foods that are not part of your everyday eating (Twiglets; ice-cream; cream and sugar on fruit) which are extra-nice because they feel naughty.

The recipes in this chapter can easily be scaled up for a couple more people, or reduced for one. Eating alone is hard to do well and requires attention but it is worth making an effort, once in a while. Treating yourself every now and then is an immediate form of self-respect as you are slowing down the pace and taking care of yourself instead of the usual gobble-and-go. Find foods that are ready-to-eat or take longer to eat than they do to cook so that you do not feel over-worked. Eating fish on the bone forces you to take your time, as do fiddly fruits such as mangoes and pineapples, shell-on prawns, crab and cutlets.

The best part of eating alone is that you can make a complete mess, eat straight from the saucepan if you like, and lick your plate with nobody there to disapprove. And leave the washing-up until tomorrow.

Quail Egg, Asparagus and Parma Ham Salad

I cooked this as a rich starter for a friend's birthday without any salad leaves but you could serve it with something like baby spinach, rocket, lamb's lettuce or some spicy Japanese greens to turn it into a main course.

Serves two as a light main course, or two to three as a substantial starter

quail eggs	:	8 (or 2 chicken eggs)
asparagus tips	:	10
Parma ham	:	70g
baby spinach leaves or other leaves (optional)	:	handful

Vinaigrette

sugar	:	small pinch
mustard	:	½ teaspoon
wine vinegar	:	½ teaspoon
olive oil	:	2 tablespoons

1   Put the quail eggs in a pan of water. Bring to the boil and cook for 3-4 minutes. Put the eggs in cold water until cool enough to handle. (If using chicken eggs, cook for 10 minutes or until hard-boiled.)

2   Meanwhile, steam the asparagus tips until tender. Cut the Parma ham into strips.

3   For the vinaigrette, mix the sugar, mustard and vinegar together in a cup or small bowl, using a fork. Whisk in the olive oil.

4   Shell the quail eggs and cut in half (cut chicken eggs in quarters). A tip for peeling fiddly quail eggs is to roll them on a work surface to crack the shell all over so it comes off in larger pieces.

5   Arrange the eggs, Parma ham strips and asparagus on two plates and drizzle over the dressing. Season with black pepper.

COMMENTS

Alice: Delicious. Expensive. Would be nice with some cold potatoes as well. Added a little sesame oil to the vinaigrette, some baby spinach and a bit of Parmesan.

Steak with Rocket Salad and Baked Sweet Potatoes

It is very easy to buy the ingredients for this dish and turn up at a friend's house to cook them as a treat with an extra-nice bottle of red wine.

Serves two

sirloin or rump steaks : 2 x 170-200g
sweet potatoes : 2
ripe tomatoes : 6
spring onions : 2
rocket : small bunch

Dressing

white sugar : scant ½ teaspoon
vinegar : 1 teaspoon
olive oil : 1½ tablespoons

1   Preheat the oven to 190°C fan oven/200°C or 400°F electric oven/Gas 6.
2   Put the sweet potatoes on a baking tray and put in the oven for 45 minutes or until cooked.

3   Meanwhile, slice the ripe tomatoes. Slice the spring onions. You can stir-fry them in a trice if you do not like raw onion or brush the whole spring onions with oil and wilt on a griddle pan and then cut them into lengths. Mix the onion and tomato with the washed rocket.

4   Make the dressing by mixing the sugar with the vinegar and whisking in the olive oil with a fork. Season with salt and pepper.

5   Cook the steaks as you like them (rub with oil and season each side with salt and pepper, first), and serve with the tomato salad and sweet potatoes.

COMMENTS

Katherine: Baked sweet potatoes are good and I gave some to James (aged one year and two months) the next day with some tuna fish.

Betty: A few drops of Worcestershire sauce make a delicious seasoning for baked sweet potatoes.

Dover Sole with Lime and Soy Sauce

Fish does not always have to be with 'delicate' sauces: it can take strong flavours such as chilli and soy sauce.

Other 'treating' fish, apart from sole, include monkfish tail (400g for two) or snapper. For a more everyday dish, you can use whatever white fish fillets are cheapest that day. If they are thin fillets, roll them up loosely, to ensure they cook evenly, and bake for 10-15 minutes. Serve with courgettes and potatoes.

Serves two

Dover sole : **2 x 250g (as a big treat) or**
1 x 380g, on the bone
garlic : ¼ clove
lime : 1
soy sauce : 1 tablespoon
red chilli (optional) : ¼

1   Preheat the oven to 220°C fan oven/230°C or 450°F electric oven/Gas 8.
2   Put the fish in an ovenproof dish, dark-side-up, and slash this side five times diagonally so the cut goes right through the flesh of the top side of the fish (but not through the bones).
3   Crush the garlic and spread into the slashes. Squeeze the lime and pour the juice and soy sauce over the fish. If using, cut the chilli into small pieces and put in the slashes. Cover the dish tightly with foil.
4   Bake for 15-20 minutes or until the flesh is cooked through.

COMMENTS

Alice: I now need soy sauce with sole and rice like I need ketchup with cod and chips. Ate it with M&S sole *goujons*. Has to be with white fish: not so good with salmon.
Liz: Used rolled-up plaice fillets. Delicious. Liked the combination of flavours (and used chilli). The eating process was slowed down, and therefore savoured, by having to remove fish skin whilst eating.

Stir-fried Parsnips with Apple Juice

Parsnips are too good to eat them only with a roast. This stir-fry dish goes with pork chops, chicken or game and can be made slightly in advance and reheated just before serving. I have made a couple of batches for a dinner party but you mustn't crowd the pan or they do not cook properly.

Serves two

parsnips : 2 medium/about 300g
olive oil : ½-1 tablespoon
apple juice : 2 small wine glasses/200ml

1   Peel the parsnips and cut into thin, 3cm long batons. They must be thin to cook through properly.
2   Heat a little oil in a frying pan or wok. Add the parsnips and cook, stirring often, for 5-8 minutes or until well on their way to becoming tender and patched with brown.
3   Add the apple juice, turn down the heat and cook for 6-8 minutes or until the liquid has reduced to a slightly sticky sauce and the parsnips are cooked.

COMMENTS

Mark and Isa: Absolutely delicious and very original. Would be very good with pork. Lovely, appetising smell wafted around the house when we cooked this.

Banana Mush

Enjoyably infantile. Assemble it for yourselves, indulging in a little mess-and-mush therapy, and eat curled up on a sofa after a hard day or on a Sunday night.

Serves any number

bananas : 1 per person
digestive biscuits : 1 (plain or chocolate) per person
cream, double, single or clotted : according to greed
brown sugar : 1-2 teaspoons per person

1 Using a fork, mash up a banana in each bowl.
2 Crumble the digestive biscuits (for extra luxury use chocolate digestives) and mix with the bananas, cream and brown sugar.

COMMENTS

Debbie: Make this if anyone ever accuses you of being an adult.
The way to get within the child within.
Alex: I licked my plate. Comment from son Thomas (aged four months) on his version, with pear: 'Fun to regurgitate.'

Supper from a Corner Shop

CARAMELISED ONION TART
HOT CHOCOLATE SOUFFLÉS

Serves four

THIS IS A CANNY MEAL for when you want to cook something delicious but cannot face the screaming toddlers and queues in the supermarket at a weekend. Everything in this meal should be available at a bog-standard corner shop.

What are the most basic ingredients available anywhere? Onions, eggs, cheese, milk, butter, flour, sugar and chocolate. Use the egg yolks to make a rich topping for a tart filled with slow-cooked, caramelised onions and whisk up the egg whites for hot chocolate soufflés.

Tarts and soufflés are very useful techniques for transforming any old ingredient into something good. Bits of pepper, spinach, broccoli ends, tins of tuna and so on can be put in a tart case, covered with eggs and milk, scattered with cheese and turned into supper for four or more. The ingredients of a soufflé couldn't be more simple yet the end result is a molten cloud from heaven.

Caramelised Onion Tart

Serves four

onions : 4-5 medium/about 700g
olive oil : 2 tablespoons
egg yolks : 6
milk : 150ml/¼ pint
Cheddar cheese : 50g

Pastry

unsalted butter : 100g
plain flour : 175g/plus extra for rolling
water : 3 tablespoons

1 Cut the onions in half, peel and slice finely. Put in a large heavy pan with the olive oil (and a bit of extra butter, if you like) and cook for the first 10 minutes over a medium heat, stirring often. Then turn the heat down and cook, very slowly over a low heat, for 45 minutes. It is very important to stir them from time to time so they do not burn. Slow cooking the onions makes them deliciously sweet. You want to end up with a thick, sweet, golden mass.

2 While the onions are cooking, make the pastry case. I prefer to make pastry by hand, because (a) I like getting my hands into food, (b) you get

a slightly lighter result and (c) you get to know the feel of how much liquid the pastry needs (about 2-3 tablespoons in this case). But if you are feeling nervous or rushed, you can use a food processor using the following method.

Chop the butter up and put it in a food processor with the flour and a pinch of salt. Pulse the machine briefly, for about 3 seconds, until the butter has been chopped up into small pieces. Add the water. Whizz very briefly, for another 3 seconds, stopping well before the pastry starts to form clumps on the blade. Take the blade out of the food processor bowl and bring the pastry together in your fingers.

3   Flour a work surface and a rolling pin. Roll out the pastry using short rolls and moving the pastry around to check it is not sticking to the surface. Instantly remove any pastry that sticks to the rolling pin (or it will stick to the dough) and keep everything well floured. Put the pastry in an 8 inch (20cm) loose-bottomed tart tin, plugging any gaps.

4   Put the pastry case in the fridge for 30 minutes. This helps to stop the pastry shrinking away from the tin and cracking in the oven.

5   While the pastry chills and the onions continue to cook (do not forget to give them a stir from time to time), separate the eggs, putting the whites into a large bowl, ready to whisk up for the soufflés, and the yolks into a medium-sized mixing bowl. Be careful not to get any yolk in the whites or they will not whisk up properly. If you are feeling very rushed, it is not a bad idea to crack each egg over a small bowl or mug and then pour the white into the bigger bowl.

6   Mix the egg yolks with the milk and season with pepper and a little salt.

7   Grate the cheese.

8   Preheat the oven to 190°C fan oven/200°C or 400°F electric oven/Gas 6. Take the tart case out of the fridge. Put some tin foil over it and completely cover the bottom of the tart with some clay baking 'beans'. You can improvise baking beans with dried beans (kidney beans or chickpeas) or a 1cm layer of rice which you can re-use whenever you make pastry.

9   Put the tart tin in the oven for 25 minutes, to partially cook the pastry. If

necessary, take the foil and beans off and cook for a further 5 minutes or so to dry out the centre of the base.

10 Take the pastry case out of the oven and turn the oven down to 170°C fan oven/180°C or 350°F electric oven/Gas 4. If there is any sign of cracking in the pastry, patch it up as best you can and put some foil tightly under the bottom of the tin to stop all the liquid leaking out (you can re-use the foil that contained the baking beans) and put it on a baking tray. Spread the slow-cooked onions over the base. Pour the egg and milk mixture on top. Scatter over the cheese. Put in the oven for 30 minutes, until the top has browned.

11 Serve with something like spinach (the best option from corner-shop freezers) and baked potatoes, or a dressed green salad.

COMMENTS

Mark: Put a big dollop of grainy mustard in the pastry case and Parmesan and Cheddar on top. Nice golden brown top and the golden onions are deliciously sweet.

Hot Chocolate Soufflés

It is a good idea to pour some cold cream into the centre of each soufflé after the first spoonful, if you have some in the fridge. Unfortunately, corner shops often seem to have only UHT cream which is no good at all. You can also buy frozen double cream in little blocks which is a good freezer stand-by for such an occasion.

Serves four

plain chocolate : 150g
caster sugar : 3 tablespoons
egg whites : 6

1   Melt the chocolate, broken into squares, in a microwave or in a bowl set over a bowl of boiling water. Stir in the sugar.
2   Whisk up the egg whites until forming peaks and put in the fridge until ready to finish the pudding. It is worth doing this in advance, perhaps when the onion pastry case is cooking, as it means less work between courses.
3   Grease four ramekins or one soufflé dish with butter if you want to stop the soufflé sticking and creating a washing-up chore.
4   After the main course, heat the oven to 180°C fan oven/190°C or 375°F electric oven/Gas 5. Re-whisk the whites until stiff (some of the white will have become liquid again). Reheat the chocolate if necessary to melt. Whisk the melted chocolate into the whites.
5   Put the mixture into the greased ramekins so that it comes right to the top of the ramekin. Put on a baking tray and cook for 8-10 minutes so the centre is slightly wobbly.
6   Serve immediately, with a warning about the hot ramekins.

COMMENTS

Susan: Exquisitely chocolatey but not as heavy as most chocolate recipes. Used Bourneville and so did not need sugar. Stirred Amaretto into melted chocolate.
Mark: Someone suggested adding chopped hazelnuts to the soufflés. One trouble-shooting point: my chocolate got very stiff when reheated so I loosened it up with some Amaretto.

LONG SUNDAY LUNCHES

Sunday is the day when many people feel free to indulge in a very long lunch, particularly when the outside world shuts down on a dim winter's day or, conversely, on long summer afternoons when you can sit outside in the sunshine.

In a really lazy version of Sunday lunch, the cook gets out of bed shortly before midday for a Bloody Mary after 1pm and food at 2pm. The meal stretches out through late-afternoon cups of tea as everyone picks away at the remnants of a rich pudding and then the hard-core get second wind at 7pm and open more bottles of wine and watch *Coronation Street* with scraps of meat and cheese. People come and go, time passes and the whole event floats freely away from the everyday.

A more traditional, easy-going mode involves *The Archers* omnibus and lots of custard. Sunday lunch is the comfort zone of our national subconscious and, as such, the ultimate one is made by your mother and includes a good pud. I like walking from the tube station to my parents' house in Ealing, where the streets have that Sunday stillness and successive houses give out smells of roast beef, roast pork, roast lamb, roast chicken and, best of all, roast potatoes. It's enough to make a Bisto Kid of the hardest cynic. Of course this is an idyll of old England. In my own neighbourhood, Highbury, the streets are full of people grabbing pints before Sky-televised football or coming back from exercise classes, and car fumes compete with curries and McDonalds. Back in my flat, though, I can always draw happiness from a deep well of nurture by making a Sunday roast.

There are ways to adapt the format to suit a modern lifestyle. Find recipes for food you can put in the oven and forget about while you wade through the Sunday papers or go for a walk. The mulled lamb stew and rich rice pudding (see pages 32 and 100) are the sort of slow-cooked dishes to put in the oven together and leave until you are ready for a warming winter lunch. Vegetables other than potatoes are delicious roasted. Try beetroot, carrots, parsnips and chunks of squash tossed in oil and cooked with the meat.

The family unit is not always at hand when you fancy an old-fashioned tuck-in. Rack of lamb and lamb shanks and smaller birds like pheasant, partridge and guineafowl are good for small numbers. Roast beef and gammon are so delicious cold that it is worth getting a bigger joint than necessary so you can make it last for three meals, roast the first day, cold the next and cottage pie or hash the third. Add some of the traditional sauces (Cumberland sauce or mustard for gammon; redcurrant jelly for lamb; horseradish for beef) and spare gravy to give leftover-meat dishes a bit of oomph.

One advantage of having so many bits and pieces at a Sunday lunch is that you can serve it to meat-eaters and vegetarians at the same table. My main tactic is to have a really good stuffing (I prefer this term to 'nut loaf' with its dire-brown-stodge connotations) which acts as centre-plate for the vegetarians and supporting-role for the meat-eaters.

Sunday lunch puddings are a chance for the Best of British. It is the puds that really stand out in our national cuisine. Even the French deign to admire custard and call it *crème anglaise*. The proper stuff is easy to make and you can listen to the radio or talk to someone as you stir.

This chapter has some pretty gutsy puddings, including one sweet-shop fantasy. If you do go for broke, let people help themselves or be careful to serve them according to appetite. They generally have seconds or thirds as the meal stretches out and it is good to watch greed grow and spread around the table as the afternoon goes on. Put some fruit on the table as something else to pick at.

Sometimes just a fruit dish or a magnificent wobbly jelly made from fresh fruit juice is more tempting than a big pud after a rich meal of roast meat. Leaf gelatine makes short work of a jelly, or you can use agar flakes, available at health-food shops, for vegetarians.

A prime bonus of the Sunday roast is the opportunity to make stock from the bones. Nothing sums up the thrifty *bonne femme* satisfaction of good cooking so much as making chicken stock. This liquid gold, its colour further enhanced by onion skins, can bubble away on the hob in the afternoon or evening, storing up goodness for the week ahead.

Roast Chicken with Roasted Garlic and Wine Gravy

This is for those occasions when two of you want the comfort of a Sunday roast but do not want to cook a whole bird. Use breast or leg portions according to preference.

Serves two

chicken quarters : 2
wine (red or white) : 1½ small wine glasses/150ml
water : 1½ small wine glasses/150ml

garlic : 4 cloves
soy sauce : ½ tablespoon

1   Preheat the oven to 190°C fan oven/200°C or 400°F electric oven/Gas 6. Season the chicken with salt and pepper. Put the pieces in a roasting tin with the wine, water and unpeeled garlic cloves. Put in the oven for around 30-40 minutes (breast quarters), 40-50 minutes (leg quarters), or until the chicken is properly cooked. To see if it is cooked, stick a knife into the thickest part and check that the juices run clear. Breast portions take slightly less time than leg portions.

2   Put the chicken on two plates.

3   Stir the soy sauce into the gravy and season with pepper and a little more salt, if necessary.

4   Pour the gravy over the chicken and serve with vegetables, potatoes and roasted garlic. Squeeze the garlic pulp out of the skin and spread over the meat as a delicious, mildly garlicky paste.

COMMENTS

Rachel: Ate it with the stir-fried parsnips and added balsamic
vinegar to the roast new potatoes at the end of cooking.
A thin gravy, that you could thicken.

Lamb with Roasted Roots

Roasting meat is simple: it is the trimmings that take the time. But you can cut out a great deal of the last-minute fuss by roasting mixtures of vegetables with the meat. Various combinations work well. Sliced fennel, peeled and quartered red onions and new potatoes is one good mixture.

Serves six to seven

leg of lamb : 1, about 2.5kg
red wine : 1½ small wine glasses/150ml
water : 3 small wine glasses/300ml
rosemary (optional) : few sprigs
redcurrant jelly : 2-3 tablespoons

Roasted roots

carrots : 10 medium/700g
parsnips : 4 medium/600g
new potatoes : 1.5kg
olive oil : 2-3 tablespoons

1 Preheat the oven to 190°C fan oven/200°C or 400°F electric oven/Gas 6.
2 Put the lamb in a roasting tray. Season the meat with salt and pepper. Put in the oven for 1 hour 40 minutes (I'm allowing 20 minutes per 500g).
3 Meanwhile, peel the carrots and parsnips and cut into chunks. Wash the potatoes. Put all the vegetables in a roasting tray. Pour over the olive oil and season with salt and pepper. Turn the vegetables so they are coated in oil.
4 Put the vegetables in the oven for an hour, turning half-way through cooking.
5 When you turn the vegetables, pour the wine, water and rosemary around the roast to make gravy.
6 Take the meat out of the roasting tray and leave to rest while you make the gravy. Get rid of the rosemary sprigs. Put the roasting tray on the hob and stir in the redcurrant jelly. Taste and season with more jelly, salt and pepper if necessary.
7 Cajole someone else into carving the meat. Pour the gravy over the meat and serve with the root vegetables and/or some green vegetables.

COMMENTS

Susan: I never realised you could cook new potatoes like this.
Mine were tiny and with skin intact, truly delicious.
Tip: Add a teaspoon or two of honey to the olive oil.
Mum: You can also make a roasted vegetable ratatouille at the
same time, using red onions, courgettes, red peppers, aubergines and
tomatoes. Cut them all into chunks, pour over some olive oil,
season with salt and pepper and roast with the lamb. Stir in
a tablespoon of balsamic vinegar at the end.

Substantial Vegetarian Stuffing

How do you include vegetarians in the Sunday roast feast? Make a stuffing that is so delicious that everyone will want a little bit with their meat but the vegetarians will get the lion's share. You can vary the dried fruit and herbs to suit the roast: prunes for beef and game; apricots or dried pears for pork or lamb. It can be made or prepared in advance and reheated or cooked with the meat.

Serves six as a side dish, four as a main course

onions :	2 medium/about 300g
olive oil :	1 tablespoon
dried wild mushrooms :	20g
bread :	3-4 medium slices/100g
prunes (dark meat) or dried apricots or pears (light meat) :	8
cashews :	100g

fresh herbs : various (e.g. 8 basil leaves and
handful flat-leaf parsley)
bought peeled, cooked
chestnuts : 200g
eggs : 2
lemon juice : 2 tablespoons

1   Chop the onions finely and cook gently in the oil until soft. Put
    the wild mushrooms in 100ml warm water and leave to soak for 10
    minutes.
2   Cut the crusts off the bread and put the bread in a food processor bowl
    with the dried fruit, cashews and herbs. Whizz until the bread turns to
    crumbs and the other ingredients are chopped up. Add the chestnuts and
    whizz for a second to get a coarser chopped texture.
3   Mix the breadcrumb mixture with the softened onions in the pan. Season
    with salt and pepper. Cut the soaked mushrooms into smaller pieces and
    add to the mixture.
4   Add the beaten eggs and lemon juice and enough mushroom soaking
    liquid to bind the mixture. Put in a medium-sized greased ovenproof tin
    or loaf tin and cover with foil.
5   Cook with the roast in the oven (at 190°C fan oven/200°C or 400°F
    electric oven/Gas 6) for 45 minutes, taking the foil off in the last 10 min-
    utes if you want to brown the top.

COMMENTS

Monica: Used double the quantity of dried mushrooms by
mistake which was fine. Good vegetarian option.

Mashed Brussels Sprouts

An interesting variation on plain sprouts and one that appeals even to people who do not like them. Delicious with chicken or game. For a de-luxe version, add an onion and 3 rashers of streaky bacon that have been chopped and fried.

Serves six

potatoes :	2 medium/400g
Brussels sprouts :	1kg
onion (optional) :	1
streaky bacon (optional) :	3 rashers
olive oil (optional) :	1 tablespoon
cream/milk :	150ml/¼ pint
nutmeg (optional) :	to taste
lemon juice :	good squeeze to taste

1   Peel the potatoes, and cut into smallish pieces. Put in a pan of water, bring to the boil, and simmer until tender.

2   Prepare the sprouts by cutting off the stalks. Some cut a cross in the bottom to make them cook evenly but I'm from the school that thinks it doesn't make much difference.

3   Cook the sprouts in boiling water for 4-6 minutes or until tender.

4   Meanwhile, peel and chop the onion, if using. Chop the bacon, if using, and soften with the onion in the olive oil for 5 minutes.

5   Put the potatoes, sprouts, bacon and onion mixture, and milk in a food processor bowl. Grate a little nutmeg into the bowl, with some black pepper and salt and a squeeze of lemon juice. Whizz to a mash. Taste and adjust seasoning if necessary.

Monica: Fantastic. The way to eat these funny things.
Good the next day on bread.
Frances: I liked the delicate green colour of the purée. Took quite a
lot of salt and pepper. The onion added good extra flavour.

Dressed Leeks

A very useful dish that can be made in advance and complements salmon,
chicken, lamb or pork or is a good part of a vegetarian *mezze*.

Serves six, as a side dish

leeks : 6 medium/about 900g
sherry or balsamic vinegar : 1 teaspoon
orange juice : ½ orange/2 tablespoons
nut oil or olive oil : ½ tablespoon

1   Trim the leeks of the coarse end of the green part. Cut into thin strips,
about 8-10cm long. Steam for about 5-7 minutes, or until cooked.
2   While the leeks are cooking, mix the sherry or balsamic vinegar, orange
juice and oil in a serving dish. Season with salt and pepper.
3   Add the leeks, toss in the dressing and serve warm or at room temperature.

Gigi: Simple but feels special. Ate them with rice and cheese.
Would be good with fish or alongside red cabbage.

Monica: Lovely. Good the next day, too. This amount of leeks took 12 minutes to cook in my steamer.

Apple and Treacle Pudding

Apple purée below and treacle tart on top. Eat with clotted cream for extra indulgence. You could add the grated rind of a half lemon to the topping, if you want to cut through the sweetness.

Serves six

cooking apples :	3 large
water :	1 small wine glass/100ml
white bread :	8 medium-thick slices
golden syrup :	1 x 454g tin
lemon (optional) :	grated rind of ½

1   Preheat the oven to 170°C fan oven/180°C or 350°F electric oven/Gas 4.
2   Quarter, core, peel and roughly chop the apples. Cook with the water in a saucepan with the lid on for about 5 minutes or until the apple collapses. You can add sugar at this stage but I like the contrast between the sharp apple and the sweet treacle top.
3   Put the apple purée in an ovenproof dish. Bear in mind that the apple will puff up a bit in the oven so the mixture should not come more than half-way up the dish.
4   Make the breadcrumbs by taking the crusts off the white bread and whizzing the bread up in a food processor.
5   Gently heat the golden syrup to make it more liquid. Put the bread-crumbs in the pan and mix with the syrup. Add the grated lemon rind at this stage, if you want.

6   Spread the syrup topping over the apples. Put on an oven tray (just in case
     it puffs up and comes over the dish) and cook in the oven for 20 minutes
     or until lightly browned.

7   Serve hot or warm with cream or custard.

COMMENTS

Gigi: Pears make a good alternative to the cooking apples
and you can use up unripe pears, like the early droppers from
Mum's garden which taste fine when they are cooked. They take
a bit longer than the apples to cook initially and, like the apples,
must be carefully cored.

Emily: You could add cloves or cinnamon to the apple and
lemon rind to the breadcrumbs.

Ed: Very good and blissfully pastry-free. I made the mistake of
serving it with ice-cream which was too rich. Real comfort food.

Ginger and Pear Trifle

I've heard trifle being described as 'English *tiramisu*' which shows how
jumbled up our food cultures have become. It remains one of our most
glorious puds. Easy to make in advance of a meal, this one uses ingredients that can be kept in the fridge and storecupboard.

Serves four

gingerbread or sponge : 4 thick slices
sherry or ginger wine (optional) : 4-8 teaspoons
jam, ideally rhubarb : 4 tablespoons
tinned pears : 4 halves

ready-made custard : 150ml
whipping or double cream : small pot/150ml
preserved ginger : 1 bulb

or

nuts : a handful

1. Put the gingerbread or sponge in the bottom of a small serving dish or into four glasses or small bowls. Gingerbread works well in this trifle but you could use Madeira or any other sponge.
2. If you want a boozy trifle, pour the sherry or ginger wine over the cake in each bowl, splashing less or sploshing more, as your tastes desire. Spread with the jam (rhubarb jam is delicious with gingerbread if you have it, but anything will do).
3. Slice the tinned pear halves and put on top of the jam. Spoon the ready-made custard on top of the pears.
4. Whisk up the cream and spread it over the custard.
5. Decorate with finely chopped preserved stem ginger or some nuts. Keep in the fridge until ready to serve.

COMMENTS

Becca: This is like a delicious cross between trifle and Christmas pudding. Used plenty of brandy which I put on the cake and then on the pears, in case I didn't have enough.

Mum: Ate this for supper with neighbours and we liked it very much. Used nuts on top, which are definitely better than grated chocolate.

Harlequin Chocolate Bar Cake

The ultimate fridge cake that allows you to play around with your sweet-counter favourites. Buy slightly more sweets than given in the recipe, for obvious reasons. These are my favourites and they give the cake a colourful 'harlequin' cross-section.

This is the sort of pudding that cannot be beaten in one fell swoop but should be left on the table at a long, boozy Sunday lunch with a large bowl of cherries or grapes and picked at during the afternoon with coffee and a glass or two of port or pudding wine.

Serves six to nine, according to greed

plain chocolate : 150g
butter : 30g
milk : 120ml
rum (optional) : 1 tablespoon
Maltesers : 80g
Bounty bars : 3
Crunchies : 4 mini or 2 standard
Mars Bars : 3 mini or 1½ standard

1   Melt the chocolate with the butter, milk and rum either in a pan over a low heat, taking care it does not overheat, or in a bowl set over (but not touching) a pan of boiling water.

2   Put the Maltesers in the bottom of a loaf tin (about 500ml in capacity). Line the sides of the tin with the Bounty bars on their sides, two halves on each long side and one half at each end. Wedge Crunchies and Mars Bars into the middle.

3   Pour over the chocolate mixture. Tap the tin firmly on the work surface to get the chocolate to the bottom. Put in the fridge.

4   When you are ready to eat the cake, dip the bottom of the tin briefly in very hot water. Slide a knife around the sides. Turn out on to a serving dish and put on the table with a serrated knife for people to cut off hunks (it does not slice smoothly like a terrine and in any case a whole slice would be sickly for some: this is a pudding that goes according to greed).

COMMENTS

Al and Katie: Served it at a long Sunday lunch with ice-cream and watched the greed spread around the table as people moved towards it. One of the guests was on a pre-wedding diet. She resisted initially . . . and then gave in. Made it with a Mars party pack.
Petra and Paddy: You don't want to know. The memory is still too fresh, and too shameful.

MAKING A MEAL
OUT OF BREAKFAST

W HEN YOU THINK ABOUT IT, breakfast is a curious meal, with its own conventions, timing and dishes. At what other time could you sit around a table reading papers and picking instead of eating and talking? Or choose to eat a gloppy oat soup and orange peel jam? And how curious that the body has been without food for ten hours and yet hardly feels hungry.

Weekday breakfasts are often reduced to a banana on the bus, a bagel mid-morning at the desk or coffee drunk in the bathroom. If there is space for a proper breakfast, it is at the weekend.

Breakfast is a moody time when your brain is still pillowed with dreams. Take it easy, especially if you have been out the night before. Brunch is the quintessence of a relaxed meal, an indoor picnic on a newspaper rug, with food that you can move towards gradually as your appetite recovers. Pick at a big bowl of fruit, dried fruit and nuts to restore vitamins and blood sugar levels. The fruit drinks in this chapter are good for those times when, as one tester put it, 'you feel too lazy to use your teeth'. To slay a hangover, you need stodge and a bit of fat. Bubble and squeak with bacon, eggy bread, pancakes layered with butter and maple syrup, sausages, beans on toast, bacon butties and hot breakfast BLTs are big guns in the breakfast parade.

Hair-of-the-dog does have some rationale behind it (you are suffering from alcohol withdrawal), as do exercise, liquid and nourishment. So walking to a pub for a pint of cider, a pint of water and lunch is not a bad idea. Unless a bed-grave in a darkened room seems like a better one.

For one, two or more, deli brunches can be bought on a whim, with the papers. Greek yoghurt with honey and nuts, croissants with melted cheese and chutney, nutty houmous and taramasalata, are all good along with picky dishes like olives.

Any sort of cooking for big breakfasts has to be fairly low-key if the cook is somewhat out of sync at that time of day. Fry-ups for crowds are out. One of the best fast-fodder dishes I know is to put lots of good meaty sausages in a hot oven for half an hour to let them cook on their own without having to prod them around a spitting pan forever. Provide plenty of toast and let everyone spread their slice with butter and sauces to wrap around the sausages in a DIY, roll-your-own, breakfast version of a hot-dog. Bacon can be mass-cooked in the same way for bacon butties.

Some people cannot stand fish for breakfast but it is excellent nourishment. Scrambled eggs and smoked salmon, fish cakes and buttery kedgeree ease the uneasy. Kedgeree benefits from butter. Fish cakes are a good way of using up leftover spuds and other vegetables. Smoked haddock simply has to be put in milk and cooked in a slow oven. Crack eggs into the milk for a rough-and-ready method of poaching eggs to bolster the breakfast. Salty fish is an excuse to eat plenty of that perennial favourite, hot buttered toast. The very phrase has a cosy luxuriance: the food equivalent of cashmere socks.

Porridge is formidable fuel as it releases energy throughout the morning. I go through somewhat smug phases when I eat it every day and it does work: not a hunger pang until lunchtime. But, at the weekend, how loathsome it is to look at a bowl that you *must* eat because it is so good for you! The way to make porridge appetising is to add things like blueberries, sliced bananas, cream, whisky, different kinds of brown sugar, honey and cinnamon, or to soak raisins or chopped dried fruits in the cooking water overnight.

For all these options, breakfast is still an essentially conservative meal and not the time for any shocks. Leave that to the newspapers.

Eggy Bread with a Kick

This is the quickest, easiest cooked breakfast of all: you can contemplate making it even in the most vague and muzzy state. If your eyes are open enough to look around the kitchen and make a little more effort, it is delicious with bacon and fried cherry tomatoes.

You can just cook the eggy bread on its own and add the sauces afterwards, but I like to cook them together. Tomato ketchup and grainy mustard are good on their own or combined. A 'Bloody Mary' combination, which shakes awake hungover tastebuds, is made by adding a few drops of Tabasco and Worcestershire sauces into the beaten eggs and spreading the bread with ketchup. Chutney is also good.

Per person

egg : 1
bread : 1 slice
sauces : various
butter/oil : a little

1   Crack the egg into a bowl and whisk up with a fork. Season with a little salt and some black pepper.

2   Spread the bread with whatever sauces you like or add liquid ones, like Worcestershire sauce, to the eggs.

3   Heat up some butter or oil in the pan.

4   Dunk the bread into the egg, coating it on both sides. Use a fork and make sure you dunk it properly so the bread absorbs the egg. Put into the pan, sauce-side-up, pouring any remaining egg on top (it will spill over and look like Australia or South America).

5   Cook for a few minutes on this side until patched with brown. Turn over, cooking the sauce-side more briefly. Serve hot or warm, on its own or with bacon and fried tomatoes.

COMMENTS

Alice: Very good for supper or a brunch but too much before 11 am. Chutney is my favourite addition and my mother's 'Bad Mood' dark chutney the best. [Alice's mother makes pots of chutney that are labelled according to what is in her mind at the time so Alice has pots labelled Marriage, Engagement and the names of various grandchildren.]

Bacon Benedict

Ideal for a post-party brunch or an indulgent weekend, this version of eggs Benedict omits the poached eggs because, in my experience, runny yolks and hangovers are an evil combination.

Ready-made hollandaise is different from home-made but tasty all the same. Soften it with a bit of cream if you are going to serve it with fish at another meal.

Serves four

smoked streaky bacon : 8 rashers
cherry tomatoes : 8
muffins : 4
hollandaise sauce : 4 tablespoons

1   Fry the bacon. Cut the cherry tomatoes in half and fry in the melted bacon fat for a couple of minutes, cut-side-down.

2   Cut the muffins in half horizontally. Break the cooked bacon rashers in half.

3   Put 2 halves of muffin on each plate and top each half with 2 bits of bacon, 2 tomato halves and ½ tablespoon of hollandaise sauce. Season with pepper.

COMMENTS

Helen: Served this followed by fruit salad for brunch.
So much less greasy than bacon and eggs. Be careful not to
over-do the hollandaise as it is rich.

Thick Fruit Drinks

You do not need a juicer to make wonderful, thick fruit drinks: a liquidiser will do. This one provides a restorative blast of liquid vitamin C at a brunch or you can keep it in a jug in the fridge ready to give some fruity energy after work or exercise.

Vary the fruit *ad infinitum* using roughly similar proportions. Add more juice if you want a thinner drink (the proportions in this recipe make a really thick and filling drink). A large banana, tin of pears and mango juice is another good combination.

I have used some tinned fruit for convenience and economy but you can, of course, use all fresh fruit instead.

Serves four

melon : ½ small/500g
tinned apricots in apple juice : 420g tin
orange juice : 150-450ml
caster sugar : 2-3 tablespoons to taste

1   De-seed and peel the melon. Cut into chunks. Put in a liquidiser with the other ingredients, including the apple juice from the tinned apricots. Use 150ml or a third of the apricot tin of orange juice to begin with and let it down with more if you don't want such a thick drink. If you want less sugar, add half or none of the sugar at this stage and add more to taste when it is liquidised.
2   Whizz to get a thick drink. Taste and add more sugar and liquid if desired.
3   If making in advance, store in the fridge and give a good stir before serving, if the drink has separated.

COMMENTS

Helen: Made thinner drinks for a morning-after-the-night-before brunch. A good opening gambit for that delicate moment when you're not sure whether your body is into instant rejection or a gentle winning-over.
Isa: Initially made it without sugar but did add some later. Good as a pre- or post-gym drink. Could use fresh fruit and add water but no sweetener, although tinned fruit is far more

economical. My usual is to put 2 bananas, a mango, a kiwi fruit
and a tangerine, all peeled, in a liquidiser and let it down
with some water. Daughter Lara has some of the
puréed fruit, before I add the water.

A REVIVAL OF AFTERNOON TEA

WHY HAS AFTERNOON TEA gone out of fashion? Far from being old-fashioned, it is tailor-made for the modern weekend lifestyle – give or take a few calories. The food can be made in advance or bought ready-made; it is adaptable to any appetite, from greedy children to picky eaters; it plugs a gap before a big night out so you are not wilting with hunger mid-evening; it gives a warm centre to afternoons when the curtains can be drawn at four o'clock; and, best of all, it is the opportunity to indulge in hot buttered toast, little sandwiches and sweet, sticky cakes.

Teatime is a chance to really enjoy being with friends. You are not sloshing back the wine or showing off or making sure there are enough glasses and knives. Just talking.

There is a collective mental block about baking because of the received idea that it requires you to be utterly orderly. Many recipes, yes, do require precision over quantities but the actual mixing is gloriously messy and lets you wallow in mud-pie nostalgia.

Baking often seems to be the way children first come to cooking. I certainly discovered what fun you could have in the kitchen as a child, amidst green-dyed drop scones and tins of condensed milk. Here's to anyone who lets a child play with food and scrape out the cake bowl! Baking still has, for me, an excitement and satisfaction that is different from any other kind of food preparation. It is partly the measuring and the mixing, partly the sweetness. You work away with pots and substances like a wizard in a den. Then the magical transformation of dough to food, the specially good, warm smells, and the rigorous, concentrated, greedy scraping out of the bowl as you wait for the cake to bake.

Tea would be my desert-island drink, after wine. I love the ritual of the leaves, the strainer and pouring water, the pots and cups and endless variations on a theme. Tea-bags are fine but good loose tea is a completely different experience. So is a visit to a tea-merchant's. They have an old-fashioned dignity rarely encountered in modern life, taking your order courteously and carefully, treading quietly about behind the counter and delivering your goods with the measured, accurate pace of a grandfather clock. Their wares still come in lovely paper wraps.

Fine loose tea has vastly more flavour than the average tea-bag. It does take a bit more time to make but it's a sad day when you can't allow yourself a little ponder while the pot brews.

Cucumber and Prawn Sandwiches

Egg and tomato; properly salted cucumber sandwiches; cress on brown bread spread with good butter; Marmite and lettuce: bring back the tea-time sandwiches!

Serves four

white bread : 12 thin slices
cream cheese : 50g

cucumber : ¼
prawns : 80g

1   Spread the slices of bread with a little cream cheese. You are using this instead of butter.
2   Thinly slice the cucumber.
3   On 6 of the bread slices, put 4 slices of cucumber and the prawns (use the sweet little North Atlantic prawns that have more flavour than the big tiger ones farmed in warm waters). Season with salt and black pepper.
4   Put the other slices of bread on top. Cut the crusts off (it makes all the difference), and cut each sandwich into 4 triangles.

COMMENTS

Mum: Delicious. I cut the bread quite thin and they were elegant.

Cinnamon Toasts

The sort of tea-time treat that goes with drawn curtains and a big fire.

Serves four

white bread : 4 thin slices
unsalted butter : about 30g
caster sugar : 2 tablespoons or to taste
ground cinnamon : 4 pinches (large or small)

1   Toast the bread slices on one side under a grill.
2   Spread the untoasted sides with a generous amount of butter and sprinkle

½ tablespoon caster sugar and a large pinch of ground cinnamon over each one. You can vary the amount of sugar and cinnamon according to taste. Put the toasts back under the grill until the sugar melts to a nice buttery crust. Take care the edges of the bread do not burn. Cut into fingers or triangles. Temper your greed for a little so you do not burn your fingers or tongue on the hot sugar.

3

COMMENTS

Aidan and Jenny: A sweet and tasty instant treat. The perfect comfort-food snack to offer to unexpected, drop-in friends and family, with a nice hot cuppa.
Sue: Did not have a grill so used a toaster and a hot oven.
Emily: Tried this with salted and unsalted butter and unsalted is far better. The fresher the bread the better because it has a slightly chewy butteriness like a French pastry. Good folded over so the butter drips on to your fingers.

Honey, Ginger and Chocolate Biscuits

I created these Florentine-style biscuits to put in some friends' honeymoon hamper but did not leave enough time before the wedding for the chocolate to set so I squidged them together in pairs and they became delicious sandwich biscuits instead of failed Florentines.

Makes about ten

unsalted butter : 50g
caster sugar : 3 tablespoons
honey : 1½ tablespoons

preserved ginger : 3 bulbs
plain flour : 3½ tablespoons
chopped blanched almonds : large handful/50g
candied peel : ½ small pot/50g
plain chocolate : ½ bar/50g

Preheat the oven to 170°C fan oven/180°C or 350°F electric oven/Gas 4.

1   Measure out all the ingredients, putting the butter, sugar and honey into a saucepan. When measuring the honey, dip the spoon in very hot water first to make the honey slide easily off the spoon. Gently heat together until the butter has melted and the sugar dissolved.

Chop the ginger into small pieces.

2   Stir the flour then the almonds, peel and chopped ginger into the butter
3   mixture. Dollop teaspoons of this on to baking sheets, leaving some space between them.

These biscuits burn very quickly so put them low down in the oven and
4   check them promptly after 5 minutes. They take between 6-10 minutes, depending on your oven. Take them out when they are browned but not burnt. Leave on the tray for a couple of minutes, so they crisp up, and then cool them on a wire rack.

While the biscuits are cooking and cooling, melt the chocolate in a
5   microwave or in a bowl set over a pan of boiling water (the bottom of the bowl should not touch the water).

Spread the chocolate lavishly over the biscuits and leave them to set,
6   chocolate-side-up, or sandwich them together.

COMMENTS

Gigi: Nice to give to people. They look posh but they're not so difficult to make.
Susan: They really do need a short cooking time or they burn. Excellent as *petits-fours* or with a simple pudding.

KEEPING WARM
IN WINTER

Aᴜᴛᴜᴍɴ ᴀɴᴅ ᴡɪɴᴛᴇʀ are almost the best times to enjoy British food when game, roots and orchard fruits come into season and you want to hunker down at home surrounded by good cooking smells, friends and bottles of red wine. Deep winter really closes us inside, away from rain or blank grey-white skies. Draw close to the heat and light of the kitchen with a bowl of citrus fruits brightening the table and a pot of stew in the oven. It is a time for making your own entertainment indoors and eating well: food is internal central heating.

Spices warm up the senses in mulled wine, gingerbread, Moroccan *tagines* and curries. Put nutmeg on rice pud and cinnamon, vanilla or cardamom in hot chocolate. Winter weekends at home are for slow-cooked stews of succulent meat that falls off the bone (such as the lamb stew in The Dragon to Dinner menu on page 32), pastries, crumbles and other puddings that swaddle you in a duvet of comfort, tucked in for the night.

The potato is the staple food that comforts the Northern soul. Baked with butter, sautéed in bacon fat with an aroma of garlic and chopped parsley, melting into cream as dauphinoise, cut into sluggy chips shining with dripping, roasted crisp, mashed to silk or bubbled and squeaked: spuds-R-us.

When feeding someone who is ill, cut the food into small pieces, as you do for a child: it makes it much more approachable when your appetite is down to zero. Small bowls of soup are good. Try pheasant and ham-bone broths as well as chicken. Allow the patient to follow their whims, whatever they are, to help them to eat at least something. Illness, like pregnancy, can create some very odd food moods.

Meatballs in a Rich Tomato Sauce

You can use any mince you like for these meatballs: beef, pork, veal, lamb or chicken. The breadcrumbs make the meatballs slightly lighter and make the meat go a bit further, but they are not strictly necessary. Use herbs that will go with the mince, e.g. 8 mint leaves with lamb; leaves from 2 sprigs of marjoram with beef; 6 basil leaves or leaves from 2 thyme sprigs with chicken, turkey or veal; and 3-4 sage leaves with pork. Or 2 tablespoons of parsley or coriander leaves with any of them.

Serves four

onion :	1
olive oil :	1 tablespoon
white bread (optional) :	2 medium slices
fresh herbs (optional) :	various, according to meat (see above)
mince :	350g
egg :	1
tinned chopped tomatoes :	2 x 400g tins
wine :	1 small wine glass/100ml
caster sugar :	a pinch

1   Chop up the onion. Cook for 5 minutes over a low heat in the oil, until soft.

2   Meanwhile, take the crusts off the bread and whizz the bread in a food processor with the herbs to make herby breadcrumbs, if using.

3   Mix the breadcrumbs with the mince, salt, pepper and the egg. The mixture may seem sticky at this stage but you need the egg to stop the meatballs falling apart when cooking.

4   Roll the meat into balls the size of a large walnut in its shell.

5   Take the onion out of the pan. Put the meatballs into the pan and fry for a minute or two on each side until lightly browned.

6   Add the tinned tomatoes, wine and onion to the pan. Stir around carefully, then cook for 30 minutes over a medium heat or until the meatballs are cooked right through and the sauce is slightly reduced. Season the sauce with salt and pepper and a little pinch of sugar to add some sweetness to the tinned tomatoes.

7   Serve with potatoes or spaghetti and some sort of greenery.

COMMENTS

Susan: I was amazed, considering the apparently unexciting ingredients, how rich and tasty the sauce was. Lovely with mashed potato that had been mashed with soured cream and grainy mustard. I didn't use the bread and it all stuck together fine and had a good texture.

Richard and Louise: Used coriander and minced lamb and served it with tagliatelle and courgettes.

Fruit and Nut Crumbles

Crumble is the earth-mother of all puddings. This nutty, boozy version is incredibly easy to make, especially with a food processor. If you use tinned fruits, all the ingredients can be on stand-by to warm up a day that is too cold and rainy to contemplate a trip to the shops. You can replace the fresh pears with a large and a small tin of pear halves.

Serves four to five

pears (better ripe but don't have to be) :	5/800g
brandy (optional) :	3 tablespoons
butter :	100g
plain flour :	150g
caster sugar :	100g
almonds :	50g

1 Preheat the oven to 190°C fan oven/200°C or 400°F electric oven/Gas 6.

2 Quarter, core and peel the pears. Put them in an ovenproof dish. If you want, pour over the brandy.

3 Put the butter, flour and sugar into a food processor. Whizz to get a medium-fine breadcrumb texture. Add the nuts and whizz briefly so that you get a bit of texture in the topping. Cover the pears with the mixture.

4 Put in the oven for about 40 minutes or until browned on top. Serve with cream, ice-cream or custard.

The fruit, nuts and booze can also be the following.

Plum and Walnut

12 quartered and stoned plums, 50g walnuts and 3 tablespoons port.

Banana and Pecan

6 bananas, 50g pecans, juice of 2 oranges and 3 tablespoons rum or Cointreau.

Apricot and Almond

2 x 410g tins of apricots, 50g almonds and 3 tablespoons Cointreau or brandy.

COMMENTS

Katherine: I had forgotten how easy crumble is to make
and the brandy is a good idea.
Emily: Replace half the flour with ground almonds for
another tasty topping.

Hot Buttered Rum

This is delicious served with pineapple as a pudding, or at any other time when you are cold. You can add all sorts of spices like cinnamon sticks and cloves to make it into more of a hot toddy. If making for less or more people, the basic formula is equal parts rum, orange juice and water and scale down or increase the sugar and butter in proportion or to taste. Muscovado sugar adds a dark, warm note.

Serves six to eight

unsalted butter	:	30g
sugar (white or brown)	:	4 tablespoons
rum	:	300ml
orange juice	:	300ml
lemon	:	a strip of zest
water	:	300ml
nutmeg (optional)	:	few gratings

1 Put the butter, sugar, rum, orange juice, lemon zest and water in a saucepan.
2 Heat gently, stirring, until the butter and sugar have melted. You can do this before the meal and reheat just before serving.
3 Pour into little coffee cups. If you have it, grate a little nutmeg on top of each cup. Serve immediately.

COMMENTS

Petra and Paddy: We greeted our guests off the train with tumblers of the stuff (you're right about coffee cups; in glass it reminds one of dead gravy). They were rapturous. Some said it should replace mulled wine forever; others that it tasted like melted Christmas pudding. All said they would try and remember it for Christmas. All agreed that judiciously added lemon zest makes it zing. Cousin Alex, after attempting a verse of 'Farewell and adieu to you, fair Shpanish ladiesh' embarked upon 'What shall we do with the drunken sailor?' but couldn't remember the answer.

CHILLING OUT
IN SUMMER

Countries that are either hot or cold are geared towards their climates but Britain is a glorious hotch-potch and so we change our food, like our clothes and our moods, with the weather. The progression from winter stews to summer salads gives variety to our diet and celebrates an inevitable part of being British.

Summer opens us up like cloudless skies for relaxed suppers, picnics and barbecues. Food can be lighter and makes use of the fruits and vegetables in season. Picnicking is full of anticipation and satisfaction, from opening up the picnic bag and sharing out the spoils to lying back afterwards looking up at leaves and clouds, then closing your eyes and hearing a river or birdsong and smelling the flowers and grass in the air before dropping off for a zizz.

Eating outside is liberating and it feels madly good when you have to brave the elements. Rugs can go under or over people! It is crucial to minimise cutlery and crockery. Eating with your hands is all part of the freedom from everyday rules and helps you enjoy the food more through touch and licking your fingers.

Picnic spots couple food and landscapes in images that play in my memory like home ciné films: roast beef and mustard baps on top of the Cairngorm mountains; tomato soup amidst Highland mizzle; barbecued lamb and red wine on springy heather; a squidgy, chocolate cake covered in melted Mars Bars on a tenth birthday picnic with my twin brother, a gang of friends and some nosy cows in an Oxfordshire field in June; trying eight different cheeses by the Tamar in the buttery Devon air in September.

Barbecueing is fundamental cooking: heat transforming food. Fan-ovens, woks, rotisseries, wood-fired ovens, microwaves are all embellishments on this central principle. Why do some men refuse to cook indoors but turn into Barbecue Man for a brief season in the summer? Perhaps — who knows? — because the tools of everyday cooking, from pots and pans upwards, get in the way the rest of the time, like a screen of expertise, as off-putting as jargon. If I were teaching someone to cook, I would keep it simple and start with a barbecue, rather as they did in the Stone Age.

You can get away with simplicity at a barbecue because the smoke makes plain food taste delicious. Having said that, barbecues are no longer just about hunks of meat for neanderthals. Char-grilled vegetables, firm fish like tuna and swordfish, seafood and bright salads all play their part. I veer towards lamb rather than chicken as it does not have to be cooked through and through and is good slightly pink. The Moroccan lamb recipe in the Saturday Night Showtime chapter (see page 91) is excellent barbecued. Venison and spicy *merguez* sausages ring the changes on the banger front. Marinating meat and fish does make a difference to taste and texture.

Marinated Vegetables and Haloumi Cheese

This dish is good as part of a barbecue, especially when some of the guests are vegetarian. Haloumi cheese holds its shape when cooked and is a good alternative to meat. You can also make this inside, using a grill, either as a starter or light supper dish.

Serves six as a starter or as part of a barbecue,
four as a light supper dish

red peppers : 2
orange or yellow pepper : 1
courgettes : 4 medium (2 green,
2 yellow if possible)
fennel : 2 bulbs
haloumi cheese : 250 g
red onion : 1
lemon : 1
olive oil : 4 tablespoons
mint : about 20 leaves
pitta breads : 12
plain yoghurt : small pot/150g

1   Stalk and de-seed the peppers. Cut each into 8 thick strips. Cut the courgettes into long, thin strips. Slice the fennel downward between the stalks into five or six slices. Cut the haloumi cheese (a sheep's cheese, usually found near feta in supermarkets), into long slices. Finely chop the red onion – this is for flavouring, not for barbecuing.

2   Mix together the juice of the lemon and the olive oil. Marinate the cheese, vegetables and chopped onion in the lemony oil for at least 30 minutes. Finely chop the mint leaves and set aside.

3 Before the guests arrive, if you like, barbecue or grill the vegetables, turning them over when patched with brown and tender. The fennel will take the longest.

4 Put the cooked vegetables on a large serving plate and dress with the marinade and onions. Scatter over the chopped mint leaves.

5 Just before serving, barbecue or grill the slices of haloumi on both sides until patched with brown. Heat the pitta breads up on the barbecue and serve with the grilled vegetables, cheese and a bowl of yoghurt. Let people stuff everything into the pitta, to eat with their hands, or eat off a plate with a fork, as they like.

COMMENTS

Becca: Ate it as a starter. Grilled everything before the guests arrived and put it on a big plate. The colours were amazing. Haloumi is one of my favourites, grilled until the outside is crispy. Your teeth just sink into it.

Isa and Mark: Cooked it for two as a mid-week supper. Really tasty as well as being different and healthy. Looks wonderful with the different coloured peppers and the mint. If you cut the vegetables slightly smaller you can fit more into the pitta bread. If eating as a post-gym healthy supper, be organised and lay the vegetables out on the grill before going out, to cut down on time when you come back ravenous.

Panzanella

A colourful Italian salad that can be served as a starter or a light, summery lunch dish. Keep any leftovers in the fridge for lunch or a side-salad. Once, when I had no basil, I used mint instead which was deliciously fresh.

Serves four as a light meal, six as a side dish or starter

white bread :	4 thick slices (stale or fresh)
olive oil :	5 tablespoons
garlic (optional) :	1 clove
red onion :	½
balsamic vinegar :	1 teaspoon
pepper :	1 red or 1 yellow, or ½ of each
tomatoes :	4
cucumber :	¼
basil leaves :	8
capers :	½ tablespoon

1   Preheat the oven to 190°C fan oven/200°C or 400°F electric oven/Gas 6. Cut the white bread into 2cm cubes and put on a baking sheet. Drizzle over 2 tablespoons of the olive oil and toss the bread in the oil. Bake for about 10 minutes or until lightly toasted. If you like, rub the toasted cubes with a cut clove of garlic.

2   Finely slice the red onion and mix with the balsamic vinegar and the remaining 3 tablespoons of olive oil. This is to slightly soften the flavour of the onion.

3   Seed and dice the pepper and put in a salad bowl. Dice the tomatoes and put the flesh and juice into the salad bowl. The juice acts as part of the

salad dressing. Dice the cucumber. Tear up the basil leaves. Put both in the bowl. Mix in the capers.

4   Add the onion along with the oil and vinegar to the salad bowl. Season with salt and pepper. Do not add the bread at this stage. Keep the salad in the fridge until ready to serve.

5   About 10 minutes before you want to eat, mix the bread into the salad so it absorbs the juices a little.

COMMENTS

Katherine: Capers were a really good addition.
Monica: Really nice and no problem to make.

Elderflower, Lime and White Wine Granita

This very refreshing, granular ice requires no gadgetry other than a fork. It has to be made at least a few hours before supper in order to freeze in time for pudding. Or you can make it a day or two in advance, freeze, break it up into granules and put back in the freezer where it remains grainy and ready to serve straight from the freezer.

Serves four

limes : 4
elderflower cordial : 200ml
white wine : 200ml
water : 400ml

1   The morning or night before the meal, squeeze the limes. Measure out the elderflower cordial, white wine and water. Pour everything into a shallow container. Freeze.

2   Take the granita out of the fridge 10 minutes before serving. When it has softened slightly, hack at it with a fork to break up into icy granules or shards. It feels hard at first, but soon starts to split up. You can do all this well before the dinner and put it back into the freezer where it remains in icy granules, ready to serve.

3   Serve in wine glasses or little bowls.

COMMENTS

Gordon: Strictly good.

Fresh Lemonade

Fresher, more colourful and more fragrant than bought still lemonade. Keep in the fridge and serve with ice-cubes. Add a little hint of gin, if you want it boozy.

Makes a jugful or six glasses

unwaxed lemons : 6
caster or granulated sugar : 6 tablespoons
water : 1.5 litres

1   Put the whole lemons and sugar in a big ceramic bowl.

2   Boil a kettle and measure out 1.5 litres of water. Pour over the lemons and sugar. Give it a stir around. Leave to cool for 20 minutes.

3   Remove the lemons from the bowl with a big spoon. Scrape the lemon rinds all over with a fork to help release their oils. Put back in the liquid. Leave to cool for another 20 minutes.

4   Remove the lemons from the bowl with a big spoon. Squeeze the juice from the lemons and add to the liquid.

5   When cool, put into a jug and keep in the fridge. Serve in glasses with ice-cubes and a slice of lemon.

COMMENTS

Gordon: Like summer.
Helen: Miles better than bought 'fresh' lemonade. Refreshing with a beautiful lemony taste and rich colour.

Amaretti Biscuits and Compote
48-9
Apple and Treacle Pudding 129-30
Artichoke Heart and Parmesan Salad
74

Bacon Benedict 137-8
Bananas
Banana Mush 114
OJ Bananas 30
Beans and Pulses 18, 78
Provençal Bean Salad 80
Tuscan Beans 44-5
Beef
Meatballs in Rich Tomato
Sauce 147-8
Steak with Rocket Salad and
Baked Sweet Potatoes 110-11
Bread 19
Cinnamon Toasts 143-4
Eggy Bread with a Kick 136-7
Soda Bread 63-5
Brussels Sprouts, Mashed 127-8

Cheese 11
Cheese and Fruit Platter 52-3
Cheese and Onion Quickies 60-2
Feta and Mint Salad 40-1
Goat's Cheese and *Chorizo* Tart
88-9
Goat's Cheese Salad 61-2
Marinated Vegetables and Haloumi
Cheese 154-5
Mascarpone and Berry Fool 51-2
Plums with Amaretto, Mascarpone
and Toasted Nuts 99-100
Sweet Ricotta with Peaches and
Pine Nuts 96-7
Chicken 11
with Baked New Potatoes 41-3
Chicken, Orange and Pine-nut
Salad 81-2
Plum Chicken 90-1
Poussins with Dubonnet and
Orange Sauce 69-70
Roast Chicken with Roasted Garlic
and Wine Gravy 122-3
Chocolate 19
Harlequin Chocolate Bar Cake
132-3

Chocolate (*continued*)
Honey, Ginger and Chocolate
Biscuits 144-5
Hot Chocolate Soufflés 118-19
Ice-cream and Boozy Hot
Chocolate Sauce 76-7
Strawberries and Raspberries
Dipped in Chocolate 71-2
Curries, Tarted-up 45-7

Duck with Fennel and Orange 104-5

Elderflower, Lime and White Wine
Granita 157-8

Fish 12, 135
with Baked New Potatoes 41-3
Cod with Leek and Cider Sauce
23-4
Dover Sole with Lime and Soy
Sauce 111-12
Fish Steaks with Sicilian Pepper
Sauce 93-4
Salmon Pasta Salad and Rocket
65-6
Smoked Fish Pâté 39
Wrapped in Bacon 43-4
Fruit Drinks, Thick 138-40
Fruit in Ginger and Lime Syrup 82-3
Fruit and Nut Crumbles 149-50

Ginger and Pear Trifle 130-1
Greek Yoghurt with Pecan Nuts,
Blueberries and Maple Syrup 56-7

Ice-cream
and Boozy Hot Chocolate Sauce
76-7
Tarting-up 49-51

Lamb
Lamb Chops in Spicy Redcurrant
Gravy 27-8
Moroccan Spiced Lamb 91-3
Mulled Lamb 32-4
with Roasted Roots 123-5
Leeks, Dressed 128-9
Lemon Sorbet with Apricots in Gin
and Vanilla Syrup 97-8
Lemonade, Fresh 158-9

Onion Tart, Caramalised 116-18

Panzanella 156-7
Parsnips, Stir-fried with Apple Juice
113
Pasta 18
Ever-ready Carbonara 21-2
with Parma Ham, Roasted Red
Peppers, Rocket and Truffle
Oil 75-6
with Roasted Aubergine, Tomato
and Red Onion Sauce 20-1
Salmon Pasta Salad and Rocket
65-6
Peach Melba 106
Potatoes 146
Dauphinoise Potatoes 94-6
Herby Potato and Tomato Gratin
28-9
Prawns
Cucumber and Prawn Sandwiches
142-3
Prawn Cocktail in Avocado Pears
103-4
Tiger Prawns Dipped in Chilli
Oil 68

Quail Egg, Asparagus and Parma
Ham Salad 109-10

Ready-meals 19, 45-7
Rice
Creamy Rice Pudding 100-1
Fool-proof Rice 45-6
Wild Mushroom Risotto 55-6
Rum, Hot Buttered 150-1

Sandwiches 59, 61
Cucumber and Prawn 142-3
Roasted Vegetable Rolls 62-3
Sausages
Frog-and-Toad-in-the-Hole 24-5
with Grainy Mustard Mash and
Roasted Parsnips 26-7
Scallops
Scallop, Parma Ham and Spinach
Salad 89-90
in Tomato and Saffron Sauce 70-1

Vegetarian Stuffing 125-6